Both Sides of the Border

Both Sides of the Border

Small pieces of England
Bigger pieces of Scotland

Kenneth Roy

Carrick Publishing

First published in 1998 by Carrick Publishing Ltd
2/1 Galt House
31 Bank Street
Irvine KA12 OLL

British Cataloguing-in-Publication Data
A catalogue record for this book is available on request from the
British Library.

ISBN 0 946724 43 1

Printed and bound in Great Britain by
Antony Rowe Ltd., Chippenham

Contents

"Tradition guided the country people, and they us, to the very spot; but we had only the story in speculation; for there remains no marks, no monument, no remembrance of the action, only that the ploughmen say, that sometimes they plough up arrow-heads and spear-heads, and broken javelins, and helmets, and the like; for we could only give a short sigh to the memory of the dead, and move forward."
Daniel Defoe

"England gives some scope for its best; Scotland gives none; and by now its large towns are composed of astute capitalists and angry proletarians, with nothing that matters much in between."
Edwin Muir

Small pieces of England

Preface to Part I

In the spring of 1995, the new editor of the *Observer* summoned me to Turnberry Hotel on the Ayrshire coast and made me a handsome offer – a space of my own in his newspaper every week and a fee for the privilege. How should I fill the precious space? About that important question, the new editor sounded relaxed. He more or less left it to me.

The easiest way of filling the space would have been to write a column of opinions. But I looked around and discovered that the world was full of such columns, few of them any good. Besides, I had no fixed opinions to share with the readers of Britain's oldest Sunday newspaper. "The best lack all convictions." In my case, it was not that I lacked convictions, simply that they tended to change from hour to hour.

In the end I did it the hard way. I offered to go on the road, reporting what I saw, heard, experienced, and felt. This form of reporting was much favoured by the early practitioners of popular journalism – Defoe and Dickens spring to mind at once – but has gone out of fashion, partly because it involves the exercise of an independent mind, takes the reporter out of the office for long periods, and is relatively expensive. It is also less glamorous than column-writing and exposé journalism. But it was what I most wanted to do, particularly for a paper of ideas and high principles which had always allowed its writers to prosper in freedom.

The journey was to take a year and the new editor decreed that my account of it should be published in weekly instalments under the generic title "Kenneth Roy's Britain". However, the journey lasted rather less than a year. Indeed it lasted only as long as the brief and abruptly-terminated reign of the editor himself.

In a professional sense, then, the experience was disillusioning: it finished me with the mainstream media. But in another, more personal sense, it was unexpectedly rewarding: the more I saw of provincial England the deeper my affection for it became. The journey may even subtly have affected my political consciousness, for I have been less enthusiastic about the merits of Scottish home rule ever since.

For this, the first half of the book, I have selected 18 small pieces of England from the *Observer* series. They date from the late summer of 1995 to the early spring of 1996, a period that co-incided with the terminal embarrassments of the Conservative Government. Tony Blair was already the most influential political figure in the land, though not yet elected. Yet, looking back at these pieces, I doubt whether the impressions I formed, or the conclusions I reached, have been significantly altered by events.

K.R.

The prisoners' van

Bow Street

As a young journalist in London, Charles Dickens was profoundly affected by his first experience of a familiar scene at the corner of Bow Street. About 40 people were standing on the pavement, evidently waiting for something. Dickens, wondering what it could be, asked the man next to him, who replied with laconic contempt: "Nuffin". Just then, the object of the crowd's curiosity drew up. It was "the van" – the vehicle conveying prisoners to and from the magistrates' court – and Dickens never erased the memory of its awful load of guilt and misfortune.

Every weekday 160 years later, the same scene continues to be enacted on the same spot. Stand at the corner just before 10am, and you will see the prisoners' van swing into the police compound opposite the Royal Opera House. Return a few hours later, and you will see it roll away to the cells of Brixton and Holloway. But you will probably be alone. The departure of the van has ceased to be a popular form of street theatre, and the newspapers turn up only when the van holds some disgraced celebrity. For most Bow Street prisoners, humiliation is a more private grief.

Who, then, passes through that cramped old dock in Court 1? We can discount the 10-year-old boys, "as hardened in vice as men of 50", and to a large extent the "houseless vagrants, going joyfully to prison as a place of food and shelter" of whom Dickens wrote despairingly in his story, *The Prisoners' Van*. The clients these days are not exclusively from a squalid sub-culture, but a more heterogeneous collection. Some are scarcely distinguishable from the lawyers who represent them.

In the lobby, under a sign with the word "Gaolers" printed in faded letters, two people waited pensively for the start of business: a woman, middle-aged and tastefully dressed, clutching a handbag; and a watchful, kind-faced little man. Had I been directing a courtroom thriller, I would have cast the woman as a witness.

The man rose, crossed the lobby, and approached me with a slight air of conspiracy. "Can I see your paper?" he asked in a Glaswegian accent. I handed him the *Independent*, which he read with close interest for several minutes until it was time for us to go into court. "It's OK," I said, "I've finished with the paper, you keep it." But he was insistent: I must have my property back.

In the wood-panelled gloom of Court 1, at least one of the accused would have been instantly recognisable to Dickens. She came up from the cells, a defiant figure in a crumpled red jacket, to face charges relating to her social service in the West End. With icy correctness, the clerk of the court accused her of being what the law still calls "a common prostitute". She was young and beautiful, as common prostitutes sometimes are. She pleaded not guilty to most of the charges.

"How many more is there?" she interrupted furiously. "Some of this lot have bin dealt wiv already."

"I have another eight files," murmured the prosecutor.

As she left the dock – bailed to appear for trial – I thought of the girl from *The Prisoners' Van*. "How long are you for, Emily?" screamed a woman in the crowd. "Six weeks and labour," replied the teenage prostitute, and Dickens remembered her flaunting laugh, her utter wretchedness.

It is different now. Auberon Waugh may be justified in his complaint that we are a nation of punishment freaks, but the magistrates here struck me as not only patient and wise, but merciful almost to a fault. They are as incorruptible as Henry Fielding, that most famous of Bow Street benchers, and his blind half-brother, John, who claimed to be able to recognise 3,000 thieves by their voices. Dickens would be surprised by the humanitarian instinct of their successors; if it is possible to lighten the load of the prisoners' van for the lunchtime run, these men will.

Dickens might also be surprised by the nature of the modern crime considered petty enough to be dealt with by the lowest of the criminal courts. Shoplifters, flashers, harlots and Saturday night breachers of the peace – the currency of Bow Street down the ages – mingle now with nastier bits of work to create sharp juxtapositions.

In one case, the bench ordered a young man from Billericay who had "armed himself with a beer bottle during an altercation between two male persons in a public place" to keep away from Piccadilly Circus, a condition of bail which sounded more like a reward than a penance. In the next, it called for a pre-sentence report on a pornographer guilty of supplying 182 videos and 58 magazines depicting "scenes of bodily suspenson and the use of ropes tied across the breasts and vagina". For once, the magistrate's expression betrayed slight distaste. "I am not," he said in a measured tone, "excluding the possibility of custody."

Between the predictable extremes of hard-faced pornographer and idiotic pub drunk, there are constant surprises. I was wrong about the respectable middle-aged woman in the lobby; she had not been called as a witness, but to answer a charge that she and others had controlled the movements of Brazilian prostitutes. But I was not far wrong in my instinct about the kindly Glaswegian. It took a thief to know that, in Bow Street of all places, it is prudent to return a borrowed newspaper.

His offence was, however, highly unusual. He had stolen, from a travel bookshop in Long Acre, a book and 10 maps valued at £57.18. "He apologised to the store detective," his solicitor explained, "and he has not stopped apologising since. It is a rather sad case. My client is on income support and attending college in an attempt to improve his job prospects. The maps and book relate to the United States, a country he would love to visit. He feels this is as close as he will ever get."

At lunchtime, I visited the scene of the crime and watched a disaffected assistant process the usual queue of acquiescent punters. When it came to my turn, I asked for the paperback edition of J.B. Priestley's *English Journey*. Without comment or eye-contact he punched a computer keyboard and peered at a screen. "We don't have it," he said.

"Tell me. Have you ever *heard* of J.B. Priestley?" At last the young man looked up from his machines. "No," he replied with a cold stare.

He will not be summoned before the Bow Street magistrates. He will be spared the clammy indignities of the prisoners' van. Yet, I suggest, m'Lud, that this bookshop assistant is guilty of an offence at least as serious as the theft of a book and 10 maps: he is guilty of abject ignorance. Like the kindly Glaswegian, he should be given a conditional discharge. M'Lud, it is what faces us all in the end.

Dickens would have liked to know that the Glaswegian thief was called Mr Steel and that another pleasant-looking thief that morning was announced as Mr Shallow. Some of the nicest people are recidivists.

Rabble rousers

Speakers' Corner

Whatever you do in Hyde Park, London, you must not erect a tent, play a musical instrument, wash your clothes, stage a play, or feed a pelican. Likewise, if you have ever felt an urge to interfere with a statue, you had best indulge in that curious pastime elsewhere. The list of prohibited activities posted at the entrance leaves very little to chance.

There is, however, one thing you may do without hindrance. Indeed an area has been set aside for that eccentric purpose. You may speak in public.

"Ladies and gentlemen, ladies and gentlemen," bellowed a middle-aged man with a dish-cloth on his head. Even in his khaki bags he was not entirely convincing as an Islamic freedom fighter and anti-imperialist. He brought to mind a Peter Sellers caricature.

"Ladies and gentlemen" – oh, do get on with it – "we are,

we are, we are a *tribe*." He was clutching a tabloid newspaper open at a photograph of a naked girl. "American troops in our country, half a million American troops. Ladies and gentlemen, ladies and gentlemen, who gave them the authority? Hail to the Clinton! Hail to the John Major!"

A large crowd of tourists of many nationalities smiled politely. They come by the bus load each Sunday afternoon to observe the noble practice of British democracy. As established a feature of the heritage trail as the Tower of London or Buckingham Palace, Speakers' Corner is popular enough to have its own hot-dog stand. But there are hotter dogs available for public consumption. These are the ones on the soapboxes.

"Saddam he know. The Western power. They don't do nothing, ladies and gentlemen. Saddam he wait to complete our nuclear weapon and then he face it to the Israelis." He was salivating at the prospect, yet still the tourists smiled. How much provocation would it need to awaken their numbed senses?

A tiny, circular, black man resplendent in carpet slippers pushed through the throng and gesticulated wildly at the orator.

"You have no brain!" he yelled. "You are a white monkey!"

A space was swiftly cleared. Rabble rouser and heckler confronted each other in anticipation of what used to be called in Glasgow a square-go: for a few seconds it seemed that actual bodily harm was about to be perpetrated. But just as fists began to fly, a burly fellow from the crowd pulled the protagonists apart.

The speaker returned to his pedestal. Soon he was ranting about the iniquity of a world controlled by Jews. "You ought to be arrested," said a tall, grave man carrying a Bible. But he was not arrested. He went on and on about the Jews, until finally the passive spectators grew restless and drifted away in search of fresh amusement.

It was not at all like this in 1855, when 1,500 socially-conscious citizens gathered in the park, near Marble Arch, to protest against Lord Robert Grosvenor's Sunday Trading Bill;

nor in 1866, when supporters of the Reform League, demonstrating in favour of extending the suffrage, stormed the Park Lane railings after the police barred their admittance; nor the year after that, when the Home Secretary was embarrassed to discover that, although the Crown had the right to prosecute trespassers, it had no power to prohibit a meeting in advance. A second demonstration thus went ahead, the Home Secretary resigned his post, and Speakers' Corner acquired its present reputation as a symbol of free speech.

Nor was it like this in the eloquent days of Keir Hardie and Nye Bevan. And as recently as 1993, although the rot had set in by then, Lord Soper was still capable of attracting the best hecklers in the business.

"You old windbag, Donald!" cried a voice from the crowd on the Methodist peer's 90th birthday. "I see you're being your pompous, arrogant self again today!"

"Oh dear, you are an unhappy man," Soper beamed back.

In 67 years a heckler got the better of him only once. "What about reincarnation?" he was asked. "Well," Soper said, "the last thing I would want is to be reincarnated where I would meet you all the time."

"Come off it, Donald!," the man replied. "You said that in your last life!"

Lord Soper coined a phrase to describe Speakers' Corner; he called it "a fellowship of disagreement". The fellowship has gone. In its place there has developed a shrill extremism, often offensive in content and rancorous in expression.

Of course, the Corner has always attracted a high proportion of the nation's nutters. Someone who was taken there as a child remembers a speaker declaiming that, now that we British had the bomb, it was about time we used it. Such lunacy was easily mocked, but today's fanaticism has a more threatening tone. The tub-thumpers who call for a nuclear bomb to fall on the Jews may look and sound absurd, but our laughter dies in the air when we realise that they are for real.

On a typical Sunday, you will find six or seven speakers

competing for the attention of the crowd and of the under-cover policemen with hidden cameras and tape-recorders who now mix among it. In the hour I was there, as well as the Peter Sellers character, there was an American evangelist in cowboy dress, – "For God's sake, get back to Gatwick", someone implored him – two other religious fundamentalists, a man standing on a ladder staring into space, and a young Englishman delivering a monologue on changing styles of modern dance. Though he was windy and boring, he did have the merit of being innocuous.

None of the speakers was concerned with political theory, injustice at home and abroad, world poverty, the state of democracy, or any of the good, brave causes that once so exercised the stars and supporting turns at Speakers' Corner. Listening to this abject lot, the visitor from another planet would form a dim view of our intelligence and interests and a dimmer view of our prospects for survival as a race. He might well conclude that earthly civilisation has reached its fag-end; and the alarming possibility arises that he might well be right.

I walked in the rain down a long footpath until the hateful sounds from Speakers' Corner could no longer be heard. In the distance, small girls rode big horses. Men jogged. A woman alone, weeping as she walked, covered her face with an umbrella and hurried past. Two grey squirrels chased each other, one pausing to beg for scraps. Outside the Dell Restaurant, pigeons perched in line on an old man's outstretched arms and lap. "No problem," he kept saying as they lifted the crumbs, one after another. "No problem at all." After the squalid pantomime of Speakers' Corner, this ordinary suffering life was deeply comforting. "No problem, no problem at all." If only we could be sure.

Hughie's interesting station

Stockport

A woman in Piccadilly Station, Manchester, invited me to dance the tango. I said I was not much good at dancing and, anyway, I was about to catch a train to Stockport. These protestations, though true, must have sounded feeble. She persisted. "Come," she said. So I went with her.

When we reached the dance floor – part of the station concourse had been blocked off for our amusement – she asked me to embrace a tightly-packed bundle of Habitat catalogues. There were several such bundles – I could have stepped it out with the *Financial Times*, *Cosmopolitan*, even sexy young *Socialist Worker*. The largest of the job lots were more than 6ft tall and supported by casters; inside, the pages had been replaced by electronic circuitry. You gave the thing a push and it played music.

I would dutifully have selected the *Observer* as a dancing

partner, but that paper was disgracefully under-represented by a load of old business sections too small to be hugged; I was thus denied the unusual experience of dancing cheek to cheek with William Keegan's economic commentary.

"Take *Vanity Fair*," the woman suggested. Gliding round Piccadilly station partnered by the *Financial Times*, she made it look ridiculously simple. I cuddled up to *Vanity Fair*, gave the hollow block a nudge, and listened.

"What's the problem?", she yelled.

"Not a sound."

"You're not pushing hard enough," she said severely.

It was no surprise to learn that the two fully-grown idiots dancing or not dancing the tango with piles of redundant newsprint constituted for aid-receiving purposes a "moveable sculpture" and that the enterprise had the financial support of the Arts Council. Such schemes are a minor form of what Hugh Kingsmill, the literary critic, labelled "dawnism" – the periodic heralding of false dawns or heaven on earth, in this case popular culture in public places whether the public wants it or not.

The ebullient Kingsmill, who likened human existence to a cold bath ("if you lie quite still, it is just tolerable"), has been critically acclaimed as best supporting actor in both the new books about Malcolm Muggeridge, which, by some curious chance, turned up together like a couple of overdue buses.

Muggeridge doted on Kingsmill and was much influenced by the older man's philosophy of life. He wrote:

> *I discovered for the first time that Stockport Station was full of interest. There was never any need to go sightseeing with Hughie...Either everything is interesting or nothing is...Of all the many truths I learned from him I count this the greatest – that to go searching out for what is interesting is a confession of not having detected life's interest.*

We can be sure that Hughie would have ridiculed the pantomime in Piccadilly Station. But what of Stockport Station 60 years on? I went with the purpose, if it could be called a purpose, of doing nothing for a couple of hours. I would see if life was still full of interest, and hope to avoid arrest by the Transport Police.

10.40am. The buffet.

"Yes, luvvie?"

Winnie calls all her customers luvvie. She thinks I should try a baguette. With a baguette, I am entitled to a free copy of *Today* newspaper.

"I have this friend," says a familiar face in the corner, "who is *always* half an hour late." Her plea for punctuality is drowned out by another mournful announcement over the loud-speaker. The 6.10 from Bristol Temple Meads has not yet arrived on platform 2; at this rate it must have gone via Thurso. Meanwhile, the 10.46 to Deansgate has been cancelled "due to the failure of the previous train". Blaming it on the other guy – how low can the 10.46 to Deansgate sink? The cross-country from Birmingham New Street is also full of lame excuses. We await with foreboding news of the Cock of the North.

The familiar face leaves in a cloud of cigarette smoke. "Oooh, she's got such a relaxing voice," says the woman next to me.

"Who was she?"

"I dunno. I've seen her loads of times, but I can't put a name to the face. She's going to London to do a book on tape. I'm sure she's been on *Dangerfield*. Oooh, I could listen to that voice when I'm stressed."

"You are often stressed?"

She gives me a funny look and turns away.

11.10. The ticket office.

You can reach most of England and Wales from Stockport Station. An antique BR sign announces that, from platforms 1 and 2, there are trains to Buxton, Stoke, Crewe, London – note the order of precedence – Birmingham, Cardiff, Plymouth, Bournemouth, East Midlands, Grantham, Peterborough and somewhere beginning with A. (We apologise for the failure of our shorthand note and for any inconvenience this may cause.)

It is also possible to travel hopefully to Hattersley. I

visualise a self-important borough with a *Good Food Guide* restaurant and a table permanently reserved for elderly *Guardian* columnists. The next station after Hattersley is Broadbottom.

A man borrows my pen. He makes a leisurely telephone call, and returns the pen without a word. Hughie, are you listening?

11.20. Platform 3.

The Cock of the North breezes in from Euston. Four Japanese bow curtly before a driver who is here to collect them. It has the feeling of a fairly minor mission – say, a reasonable offer to take over Greater Manchester.

11.45. Platform 2.

Suddenly, from nowhere, the mad axeman of Stockport. He has a gash across his chin, and has loosely plastered the wound with paper, now extremely bloodied. His gait is unnerving: he lurches rather than walks. With a wild eye he looks up and down the deserted track, rummages in his pockets, and finally produces a smelly old notebook.

I discover that I have not the faintest idea how to communicate with a train spotter.

"Good morning. Is this a good station for train spotting?"

"Not baaaaaaad."

"Ah. You must find the Sprinters rather boring."

"Piccadilly's b-b-better."

"I expect it is. So, um, why don't you train spot at Piccadilly instead?"

"Cos I live in Stockport."

When I returned to Piccadilly, the woman was still dancing, but was seeing someone else. During my brief absence in Stockport, she had fallen in with *Yellow Pages*. They seemed quite close. I hurried past, covering my face with *Today* newspaper. Either everything is interesting or nothing is.

Shock city

Manchester

Friedrich Engels, whose experience of working in his father's cotton factory in Manchester helped to inspire the Communist Manifesto, wondered what would become of that city's proletariat, "who owned nothing and consumed today what they earned yesterday". Present events are shaping an answer.

The "shock city" of Victorian England, which fascinated and appalled social commentators, has ceased to be the "chimney of the world", a place where "civilised man is turned back almost to a savage". You would be disinclined to accept, even at 11 o'clock on a Saturday night, that it is any longer "the entrance to Hell realised". Hell is now a smoke-free shrine to post-industrialism.

The two events, or non-events, which were exciting most attention in Manchester when I arrived would have astonished Engels by their innocuous character. They were the sale of a pub called the Rover's Return to Jack Duckworth and his wife, and the imminent result of a civic campaign to stage the Commonwealth Games of 2002.

It would have to be explained to young Friedrich, before he decided that the Communist Manifesto was not worth drafting after all, that the Rover's Return is not a real pub in which the proletariat consume today what they earned yesterday, but a scriptwriter's re-invention of the homelier Victorian qualities; and that the Commonwealth is merely the disenchanted remnant of a lost empire, meeting every four years to determine which pumped-up athlete leaps highest. He would grasp at once that both are nostalgic illusions.

Then, however, Engels might recall an encounter with a member of the urban aristocracy of 19th-century Manchester. "I have never seen so badly built a town in my life," he complained, meaning that it had been allowed to develop unchecked and unplanned. The man, having listened patiently, replied: "And yet, there is a great deal of money made here. Good morning."

That was very Manchester; it is still very Manchester. It takes a certain genius to recognise that, when it is no longer socially acceptable or economically possible to make a fortune out of sweated labour, the smart modern alternative is the commercial parody of such labour through games and entertainments which exploit a popular sentimental view of a vanished society.

Pubs such as the Rover's Return have largely disappeared as an English institution, at any rate in the cities. Writing in 1946 in praise of his favourite pub, The Moon under Water, George Orwell described its unusual combination of qualities: a side-street location and ugly Victorian architecture; regulars who went for conversation as much as for the beer (it was always quiet enough to talk); motherly barmaids; good, cheap food and draught stout; open fires; a lack of drunks and rowdies. Now, does that not remind you of Mrs Walker's local in *Coronation Street*, before Newton & Ridley insisted on modernising it?

At the end of the essay, Orwell revealed what the discerning reader had guessed already: there was no Moon under Water for him, just as there is no Rover's Return for us. It is none the less possible, since we are dealing here with the genius of Manchester, to pay an entrance charge for the privilege of touching the dartboard and leaning one's elbow against the bar. For when the fictional pub is not in use as a television set, it earns a bit on the side as a museum.

Indeed, the Rover's Return has become as much a part of the city's heritage industry as the Ragged School Museum, the Museum of Transport, the Police Museum, the Courts of Justice Museum, the Jewish Museum, the Natural History Museum, the Museum of Science and Industry, and the Manchester United Museum; no doubt they will be joined one day by the Commonwealth Games Museum.

But here is a paradox which might have amused Orwell. While Manchester's favourite meeting place is a pub without a licence, to which no real rover has ever returned, those in need of strong drink flock to a pub with the same name as his perfect local. Orwell knew of nowhere called the Moon under Water, but it has just opened in Deansgate, on the site of the old ABC cinema.

It has 8,500 square feet of drinking space, three bars on two levels, 65 staff, and an effigy of Ena Sharples; it claims to be the biggest boozer in Britain. As I sat at a long table in the middle of the ground floor, marvelling at its brisk impersonality, it was hard to imagine a pub which conformed less to Orwell's essentials; someone setting out to subvert the ideal of his personal Moon under Water could not have done a better job.

When it opened, "a gang of heavies moved in and offered their services as bouncers, refusing to take no for an answer", the *Manchester Evening News* reported. The management stood firm; the threat of trouble receded. But we have come a long way from motherly barmaids and draught stout. We have left Coronation Street far behind.

According to the paper, protection rackets are common in Manchester clubs and pubs; gangs are said to have infiltrated even the "gay village" of Canal Street, where lonely cruisers who "epitomise the drive for a truly cosmopolitan city" – this ludicrous statement is reproduced with no hint of irony – are stalked by drug barons from Salford when they are not being needlessly persecuted by the police.

Who are these gangs? One anonymous "insider" quoted by the paper says: "The police know who they are, everyone knows who they are, but they are almost untouchable." Let's hear that again. *They are almost untouchable.* If this is true, the Chief Constable should tell us why.

In a brilliant article about Manchester, A.J.P. Taylor wrote that the local businessmen did not believe in putting the needs of the majority first. "They had succeeded by their own energy; and they supposed that the duty of society was discharged if it gave others the chance to do the same." Thus the home of Friedrich Engels was also the spiritual home of Margaret Thatcher a century later. And, though chimneys no longer reek, soot no longer clings to the sturdy suits of the capitalist class, and Mrs Thatcher is an old lady now, the spirit of Manchester remains influenced by past example.

The city has become – you can take the local newspaper's word for it – "a byword for nightlife pleasures...its twilight economy has brought jobs and a new vibrancy after the scourge of unemployment". By this shrewd adaptation to modern trading conditions, the successors to the mill-owners of Victorian Manchester lure 60,000 young people into amusement palaces every weekend. "Take just 10% of them," one club manager said, "multiply by £15 each for an ecstasy tablet, and you're looking at £100,000 a week." You are also looking at 6,000 ecstasy users. Shock city lives.

On the road to Piccadilly Station, I spotted a fly-poster for a Socialist Party meeting in honour of Friedrich Engels. I hope someone reminds the audience – I visualise a small, rather depressed gathering – that it was Engels' passionate belief that the growth of Manchester, though brutish and wretched, was a necessary stage in the unfolding of modern history. That long process is not quite complete, perhaps. We have yet to see where the anarchy in the streets will lead.

Mrs Garbutt's greyhound

Castleford

"Which way to the dog track?"

"There's no dog track," said a man in Castleford.

He was wearing a double-breasted suit with a splendid maroon tie. He was almost flashy enough to be a platform speaker at the Labour Party conference.

"But," I protested, producing the greyhound racing section of the *Yorkshire Post*, "it says here..."

"I can't see," he interrupted.

"Well, believe me, it says here that the first race is at 7.30 and the favourite is California Sammy."

"You want to be in Whitwood," he interrupted.

"I do?"

"It's a long way from Castleford. Far too far to walk. Tell you what. Go to the bus station and get the first bus that says Wakefield on the front."

He directed me into Hope Street. Young people were

playing games in the hall of the Methodist Church. Another lively feature of Hope Street was the Anglers' Club. I tried the door, but it was bolted. A notice in the window said, "Barred from one, barred from all", and listed the Albion Street Working Men's Club and the Royal British Legion, as well as the Anglers' Club itself. Ah, but here was the Liberal Club, a permissive haven for those who have been chucked out of everywhere else and find themselves in the middle of the road, as Liberals do. I tried the door, but it was bolted. There's nothing quite like Castleford for giving the casual visitor a raging thirst.

Not five minutes in the town, and already I had begun to feel like next month's *Crimewatch* reconstruction. I left Hope Street – bit of a relief all round – but still no sign of the bus station. "Jesus," said a poster outside a church, "is the winning ticket in life's lottery". The streets were empty, quite empty, and it was not yet 7pm. There are lonely nights in life's lottery, sweet Jesus, when you would hug a lager lout. "Humps for 150 yards", a road sign warned.

Just past a derelict building in Albion Street ("Opening soon, £1 million night club"), I stumbled into a junk yard with a taxi office at the far end. Never mind the bus to Wakefield. I would go to the dogs in style.

"Oh," said the taxi controller, "I dunno if dog track's open."

"But it says here..."

"Ay, it's open," said his mate. "Monday, Wednesday, and Friday. I'll take you for a couple of quid."

When Labour was old enough not to have to be called new, when the shift was not a function on Tony Blair's laptop but something you toiled at for eight hours, and when Albion Street still had working men, they mined coal in this neighbourhood. Then Arthur Scargill called a great strike and declared that if it was lost there would be no more pits. This proved to have the force of Old Testament prophecy: the strike was lost; there were no more pits. Now there are Japanese branch factories and enterprise parks, and the promise of a Euro terminal at Wakefield, where the bus terminates.

The industry has gone, but there is at least one remnant of its social tradition – the dog meeting. And now a tiny confession: I have a weakness for dog meetings. I even have a track record of sorts.

At the age of 16 I got a part-time job with the *Daily Record* as a greyhound racing tipster. I was assigned to a particularly dodgy meeting. Hot favourites often performed unexpectedly badly, provoking angry rumours that they had been given pace-sapping fish suppers by their owners. There was an unmistakable whiff of corruption in the air. The dogs didn't smell too sweet, either.

"You're on the early side," said the taxi driver as we pulled into Whitwood Stadium, "but I can recommend the New Wheatsheaf round the corner. Good pint, there." I tried the door of the New Wheatsheaf, but it was bolted. "This is incredible," I said to a man in the car park. "I can't find anywhere in Yorkshire open." He advised me to be patient. He said that people came from miles around for the bar supper.

I headed back to the dog track, and read the rules of the meeting.

If in the opinion of the stewards a greyhound fights during the course of a race, it shall be disqualified for fighting.

The management reserves the right to warn off any owner, trainer or greyhound.

"Warn off" – yes, that sounded very Castleford. Barred from one meeting, the delinquent dog will quite likely be barred from the lot, though he could always try his luck at the Liberal Club.

The ground was eerily floodlit as if in anticipation of some electricity supply crisis, but there was just enough visibility to be able to check the *Yorkshire Post*'s card. And, straight away, I spotted the familiar name of Southend Ted, Britain's first Euro-sceptical greyhound, better known to his constituents as Sir Teddy Taylor. I might have had a flutter on Southend Ted, but then I realised I was looking at the wrong card: the former Scottish Office minister was running at Askern. Don't ask me where Askern is; I only hope it has been spared a Hope Street.

Anyway, here at Whitwood, we were facing a slight logistical problem. With the first race overdue by three minutes, there wasn't a bookmaker in sight.

"Tell me," I said to a fellow punter, "where have all the bookies gone?"

He gave me a withering look.

"There's no bookies," he said in a low voice, "because nobody wants to bet."

"Really? How quaint!"

"These dogs," he said, pointing to five barking hounds in the competitors' enclosure, "they're *fresh*."

Baffled by this explanation, I took a closer look into the enclosure and was struck by the youth and beauty, the sleek coat, of the one nearest to me. But this was just the owner. As for Mrs Garbutt's greyhound, who could tell? Fresh enough, one supposed. Then Mrs Garbutt said that her dog, Gambit, had never raced before, and it suddenly occurred to the former greyhound racing tipster of the *Daily Record* that it must be a novices' race. Without form, no self-respecting punter would be interested.

Some said the bookies had been held up on the motorway. At gunpoint, with any luck. But there was a unanimous feeling that they would be here in time for the fifth race. In fact, one shifty fellow appeared just before the off, and I managed to put £1 on Gambit. I got decidedly mean odds of 2-1.

Mrs Garbutt's greyhound led from the start, never faltered, and won by what the *Yorkshire Post* next morning described as half a length. Mrs Garbutt, from Pontefract, jumped for joy. I executed a modest leap myself. And then I did what sensible punters must do. I returned to the bookie, handed over the winning card, collected the loot, and walked away from Whitwood Stadium in the direction of the Four Ferrets public house. It was the only door in Castleford I had still to try.

You may be wondering what happened to Southend Ted. He finished naewhere.

On a point of order, Chair

Leeds

They threw me out of the Civic Hall, Leeds, just before the interesting part of the meeting. You know it is about to become interesting when a man called Chair announces that the rest of the business will be dealt with in private.

Earlier, a councillor had found it possible to utter the following words: "The admin staff will gain familiarity in all aspects of interrogating and manipulating the data and at this point in time, Chair, I am optimistic that we will achieve what we set out to do." This was an example of how little political language has changed since Orwell noted its distinguishing features: chronic anaemia and an absence of concrete thought.

After an hour of municipal-speak, it was almost a relief to be told that I was no longer welcome. Chair looked straight at me and said "Thank you very much", and a dozen pairs of eyes turned in my direction. Well, I left without a fight. But I wonder what I did to merit Chair's thanks. Not much, as he will discover.

By the time they evicted me, I was the last surviving visitor. Yet the public benches were pretty full at the start; there had been a queue the size of a football team for passes to committee room 6/7. This suggested a surprising degree of enthusiasm for the workings of local democracy. But the ordinary citizens who were present made it plain that it was not some dispassionate curiosity which had brought to them to the monthly meeting of Leeds social service committee, but a furious sense of injustice.

"My mother is 94 and mentally infirm," said one woman. "The old souls are happy there," said another. "At their age, it's not fair to move them," said another. These disenchanted electors had come to protest about "a decision in principle" to close Parklees Home and day centre in the Beeston district of the city, and to hear the outcome of a "consultation process" (item 23 on the agenda).

A few minutes before the meeting, a balding man with an air of authority tried to appease the punters while the elected members were served tea and biscuits at their tables. "He's the director of social services," someone muttered.

"Look," he said, "we have no intention of closing Parklees before we have made alternative arrangements for the residents."

"We're not interested in alternative arrangements," came the reply. "We want the home kept open."

"Please," the official implored, "don't get angry."

Please don't get angry. On the contrary, the frustrated friends of Parklees Home were behaving with admirable restraint. But, on a point of order, Chair, why should not the voters of our towns and cities get angry occasionally at what is done, or not done, in their name? It may be inconvenient when 11 people turn up at a meeting and risk giving the councillors indigestion – but no one forced the biscuit-eaters to stand for election. Our masters are paid for the mere act of attending such meetings. They are due a little well-directed anger.

But let that pass, Chair, for there was worse to follow. The official then risked a peasants' revolt by hinting that, although it appeared on the agenda, item 23 would not be taken. "Diabolical!" declared one man, sweeping up his papers. "You hope we'll get tired, and that next time we won't be here," another said bitterly.

"It's up to the councillors," the official sighed, as if that were the end of the matter. Quite. But here was an odd thing – there were 20 councillors in the room, including a majority aligned to that movement of universal brotherhood once known with a certain ironic affection as the people's party. Not one showed the least interest in the distress and disaffection at the back of the room. They stayed in their seats, nibbling their digestives.

Chair began with a statement peremptory in its brevity: "In order to avoid an unnecessary wait for some of the visitors, I wish to announce that item 23 has been withdrawn." No explanation; no apology. Afterwards, I telephoned the PR department to complain about this arrogant performance.

The director of social services, Keith Murray, returned my call. He said that item 23 had been withdrawn because the committee was not yet satisfied that it had met the legal requirements for consultation over the closure of the home. So why had the chairman not had the courtesy to say so plainly? Mr Murray replied: "It is not normal protocol to explain the reason for withdrawing an item." (Good heavens, why not?). He added that interested parties had been informed by letter.

In the absence of those irritating people, the voters, the rest of the meeting went smoothly. Indeed, such was the prevailing amity, it was difficult to believe that the social services committee included councillors of opposing political parties. There was not a single vote. There was scarcely a cross word. A great deal of public expenditure went through on the nod, including the grand sum of £339,000 to "refurbish" two area social work offices; suspended ceilings in the filing room are a must, apparently.

I bought the local newspapers expecting critical scrutiny of these items and an account of the outcome or intriguing non-outcome of the Parklees consultation process. But the meeting was judged too boring to be reported: as far as the people of Leeds were concerned, it might never have happened. I selected this committee at random. The alarming thought occurs to me that it could be fairly typical of how local government operates in Britain.

Near the Civic Hall is a much grander building – the Town Hall, a monument to the pride and ambition of Victorian Leeds. I went there after the meeting and landed in the middle of a tea dance. "We're going to continue now with a Broadway quickstep," said a young man immaculate in dress shirt and bow tie. "Take your partners now." A few elderly couples got up and stepped daintily to a recording of a song called Baby Face. It made a curiously poignant sound as it echoed down endless corridors.

All around the walls of Leeds Town Hall there are beautifully crafted mottoes asserting former certainties: "In Union Is Strength"; "Trial By Jury"; "God In the Highest"; "Industry Overcomes All Things"; "Forward"; "Goodwill Towards Men". Few, if any, of these precepts are untainted by post-war experience. "The trust in a caring minority weakened," wrote R.F. MacKenzie, the teacher and visionary, summing up in a striking phrase the disillusion with power structures we once instinctively accepted as benevolent.

In an age of diminishing trust and precious few certainties, we have retreated into our private lives. We no longer go to Leeds Town Hall to hear great oratory and debate great issues. Instead, we go tea dancing. We rise only for the Broadway quickstep. And on those rare occasions when we are shaken from our indifference by an imminent threat to some community asset – let us say, an old people's home – we find ourselves confronted by a secure, remote bureaucracy sipping its tea and by the shocking realisation that we voted for these people or, almost as bad, failed to vote at all.

Sad and mad

Blubberhouses and Bedlam

Until recently I was convinced that there could be nowhere in the country with a sadder resonance than those Perthshire twins, Dull and Weem. They have the forlorn ring of a pair of Sassenach comics who died one Monday night at the Glasgow Empire; they are the Mike and Bernie Winters of British geography. But then I spotted on the map of England a place-name even more inimical to joy. Lo, I discovered Blubberhouses.

Mr Walker of Station Taxis, Harrogate, scratched his head at the prospect of a fare to one of the melancholy wonders of the modern world. It was, he admitted, an unusual request.

"Where in Blubberhouses do you want to go?" he asked.

So – I hear you say – there is a *choice?* But I was ready for this challenging question. I told Mr Walker to take me to its bleeding heart.

The essential characteristics of Blubberhouses were

already clear in my mind: a most excellent funeral parlour; the Weep and Wail public house; a convalescent home for left-wing Labour supporters; the boarded-up drapery department of the Blubberhouses & District Co-operative Society; the vicarage of the Rev Jeremiah Tombs; and the offices of the Blubberhouses Bugle, the last local paper in Yorkshire with "In Memoriam" notices on the front page. The name of its football team escapes me. Let's just call it Cowdenbeath.

We headed out of Harrogate on the A59 to Skipton. "Blubberhouses 7", a road sign declared ominously.

The journey was unremarkable until we came to a waterlogged tent marked "women's peace camp". I thought of stopping for a word with these plucky campaigners, but it had begun raining almost horizontally in anticipation of our arrival in Blubberhouses, and Mr Walker said they were a bloody nuisance anyway. So we sped past the women's peace camp and drove alongside a field containing a number of outsize golf balls – I managed to count 15, but there might have been more. These balls were seriously big. They had dimples which would not have disgraced the noble chin of Robert Mitchum.

"They're listening stations," Mr Walker explained. "There were only a few to begin with. They keep building more."

The first of the golf balls arrived in the district in 1959, the year America regained the Ryder Cup. As for listening stations, most people in those days were innocently addicted to a programme for an era of full employment. They called it *Music While You Work*; I suppose the nearest equivalent now would be an incomprehensible speech by Mr Gordon Brown. I digress. In an obscure pocket of Yorkshire, uniformed chaps were listening to more sinister stuff on foreign wavelengths. For this was the local end of the Cold War. And if it had to end somewhere, they couldn't have chosen a better place.

But now the Cold War is over and they're still listening – more than ever, judging by the number of new balls. Is the sound of poor Mr Yeltsin pouring himself another whisky really so fascinating? Perhaps the listening stations are the military equivalent of the mysterious holes in the road which appear from time to time in our towns and cities.

In the Hopper Lane Hotel – no Weep and Wail, sad to relate – I asked an offensively cheerful and agreeable fellow how Blubberhouses acquired its name. There were two possibilities. Warming to the first and in his opinion more plausible theory, he showed me pictures of the local satanic mill, long ago demolished to make way for a cricket pitch, where Victorian urchins from London once slaved. After work they wept copiously in the mill houses, blubbering long into the night. People of the district heard their lonely crying and thought: Ah! So we must name it Blubberhouses!

Later, Mr Walker took us along a dirt track past a sign which said: "Blubberhouses Cricket Club. Next match Galphay & Winskley." There was no sign of the cricket club. At the end of the track, however, there was a farm. And here is a curious fact about farms: no one ever seems to be at home. I had come in search of a haunted atmosphere, some chilling presentiment, and stumbled instead on a cowpat. Pity help Galphay & Winskley on this wicket.

By a log fire in the Hopper Lane Hotel, the local historian declared himself less impressed by the second theory: that whales were brought here from Whitby for cutting-up.

"What's the snag?" I asked.

"Well, it's a helluva long way to bring a whale," he said. "Couldn't they have done the job just as well in Whitby?"

There was a rough logic about this argument; one had to agree that the London urchin theory was more persuasive. For a scholarly view, however, I turned to *The Place Names of the West Riding of Yorkshire (Part V)*. According to that well-thumbed tome, Blubberhouses may owe its name to a certain Walter Bluber, who had a house in the vicinity; equally, it may be derived from the word bluber, meaning a spring, of which there are several nearby. You now know as much about Blubberhouses as I am prepared to tell you.

I am not finished yet; nor is my friend Mr Walker. On our return to Harrogate, I offered him his second strange hire of the day. Having seen the saddest place in the kingdom, I now wished to visit the maddest.

"Proceed to Bedlam."

Mr Walker insisted at first that he had never heard of a Bedlam near Harrogate. He believed that there might be one over Durham way. When I pressed the point, he consulted a map and admitted that, sure enough, there appeared to be a Bedlam on the road to Burnt Yates. Come to think of it, he remembered from his youth a place called Bedlam Bank.

We went via Killinghall to a place called Clint, but no sign of Bedlam or its bank. At the New Inn, Clint, I asked a couple behind the reception desk if we were anywhere near our destination.

"*This* is Bedlam!" the woman replied. She was 'avin me on, though.

"We've had this before," said her partner. "Bill was talking about it just the other day, funny enough. He's not in yet. Isn't there another Bedlam?"

"Over Durham way, I understand."

"No, Scarborough, I think."

Mr Walker and I had another squint at the map. Bedlam was marked, we were to all intents and purposes *in* Bedlam, yet all evidence of its existence had gone. Mr Walker said it was his belief that it had been renamed Whipley Bank. Tory ladies will be stimulated to learn that Birch Construction Ltd is building houses near Whipley Bank. Indeed, if the Home Secretary is looking for somewhere to locate the first of his tough new penal establishments, he could do worse than consider the parole-free possibilities of this isolated hamlet.

Our mission was almost complete: but not before I had knocked at a cottage door in a last attempt to exhume some mad-eyed worthy who remembered the glory days of Bedlam. A dog barked ferociously, and I fled. Never accuse me of being an investigative reporter.

A night at the Rep

Birmingham

One of the most thrilling places in the world is the place round the corner where they are putting on a play. J.B. Priestley called it "the essential theatre" – not Shaftesbury Avenue with its neon lights, but the theatre which pops up unexpectedly in an ill-lit street of some dreary town.

Britain's essential theatre is repertory, a leaden name for one of the great humane influences of the 20th century. It was founded in Manchester 87 years ago by a fabulous character known to all as Miss Horniman, "a withered spinster clad in rich brocade", as the playwright Harold Brighouse remembered her.

The idea was quickly taken up in Glasgow, Liverpool and Birmingham, spread to most other parts of the country, and has survived two world wars, depression and recession, and the brutal competition of the electronic media. Against all odds, Miss Horniman's eccentric vision has become our theatre for all seasons.

Repertory should never be confused with touring houses which rely on hack tours got up as vehicles for minor television personalities, nor with self-conscious arts "centres" in which the auditorium is often smaller than the bar. Repertory, in Barry Jackson's phrase, "encourages a living and critical approach to the art". It is, or should be, a stage of serious ideas, big in ambition, accessible to all.

One evening recently, I thought of Jackson and his theatre, and was seized by a childlike enthusiasm that Priestley would have understood. Even at 9.30pm in my outpost of the global village, I supposed it should not be difficult to discover what was on at Birmingham Rep. First, I consulted the *Observer* listings. Not a word. Ceefax and Teletext were no more helpful. So I telephoned the box-office. It was closed, but a voice had left a message. This told me everything that a potential customer could wish to know, apart from the title of the play. So much for the global village.

I went to Birmingham anyway. Is there any good to be said about Britain's most unpopular city? Of course there is. From the Holiday Inn – two double beds for the price of one, should you ever need two double beds – it is possible to do what is normally in Birmingham a very daring thing: it is possible to walk. Stride into the nearest underpass and a minute later you will come face to face with an inspiring sight.

On the left of a handsome square is the Symphony Hall where Simon Rattle presides. He had been conducting there the previous evening (Beethoven's 9th), with most of well-doing Birmingham present. But the casual visitor has to be lucky to catch Sir Simon; he comes and goes like the night star. In any case it is not the Symphony Hall with its occasional brilliance which would have caught the eye and lifted the spirits of grumpy old Jack Priestley, but the pool of light next door. For here is Barry Jackson's Rep, splendidly re-housed, looking almost glitzy (perish the thought), but still "a place where intelligent persons can find intelligent recreation". At least, so I devoutly hoped.

Jackson established his company in 1913; next to Liverpool, it is the oldest surviving Rep in the country. A bust of the founder lurks in a dark spot near a side entrance. They should move it to a more prominent place, for Sir Barry was a noble pioneer. He believed that the theatre should "serve an art instead of making that art serve a commercial purpose". What a curious, old-fashioned notion!

This month, they are doing *The Way of the World* in modern dress: Congreve's dark comic masterpiece has been re-located in Thatcher's Britain. A few weeks ago the critics gave the company a terrible mauling for a *Macbeth* set in the year 2055, but the one endearing trait of critics is that if they are tough about something, they will usually bend over backwards to be lenient next time. So *The Way of the World* has opened to a lukewarm rather than a hostile reception.

My usual response to a modern-dress version of a classic is relief at being spared the spectacle of actors prancing around in period costumes. And the interpretation by resident director Bill Alexander feels acutely intelligent rather than gimmicky: if you choose a cynical play with a plot as thick as pea soup, and its themes are obsession with money, social disgrace, failure, desperate loneliness, ugliness, and the horrors of old age, you are quite entitled to place it in 1985.

A captivating actress from Cardiff, Rakie Ayola, plays the central character, Millamant, not as some beribboned Restoration beauty, nor as a calculating temptress, but as a thoroughly modern young woman. She delivers with luminous vitality her conditions for marriage. And because it is so sensible, and because it may even save one or two fragile relationships this morning, I will summarise her 295-year-old prescription for a successful marriage:

No calling of names (sweetheart, my dear, etc); no public exhibition of nauseous familiarity or fondness; no visiting together; no Sunday outings in the park; the freedom to pay and receive visits, write and receive letters; no obligation to be intimate with fools because they happen to be one's partner's relations; the right to dine early, late, or alone without giving a reason.

Few have heard of William Congreve these days, though by an odd coincidence that larger repertory company on London's South Bank is also presenting *The Way of the World* at the moment. It's a thin house in Birmingham. Applause at the end is muted, and the cast looks slightly downcast as it takes its bow. But Barry Jackson would have championed the notion that repertory is not about the easy commercial success. It is sometimes about the right to fail with honour.

Afterwards, I asked Birmingham's general manager – they prefer to call him executive producer – how much the actors are paid. John Stalker's answer shocked me. It is an average of £300 a week – £15,000 a year, not that anyone can afford to stay that long. After a couple of productions, most actors return to London for the commercial voice-over, the telly part, the silly work which pays decent money.

This is a pity for two reasons. It takes away one of the lynchpins of the repertory ideal – the permanent company deriving professional satisfaction from serving the regional stage – and it reinforces the metropolitan bias which so corrodes and disfigures British life. Furthermore, it is probably bad for standards; the history of the theatre shows that most great work has been accomplished by ensembles, people who have acted together for a long time.

Perhaps we should just be grateful that such a valuable and beautiful place as Birmingham Rep survives on any terms in our bracing new era of enterprise culture: that it is still possible for a stranger, alone in some unfashionable town, to stumble on the essential theatre, the place where they are putting on a play tonight. For that civilising mercy, three cheers. Better still, let's give them a standing ovation.

No place like home

Castle Vale

Disraeli's two nations, "between whom there is no intercourse and no sympathy", are no longer the rich and the poor, according to modern Conservative thinking. Nowadays we are said to divide more subtly between the independent citizen, who owns property and earns a living, and the dependent sub-class which is either "trapped in the safety net" or, less charitably, "sponging off the state".

This stratification of British society is widely accepted, even by many non-Conservatives. There is a popular belief that poverty – "real poverty" – has disappeared. But has it? I took a bus and an open mind, and a book by Beryl Bainbridge, to Castle Vale estate on the outskirts of Birmingham.

In 1969 – the year before the fall of Mr Wilson's first government – 20,000 people were moved there from the

Edwardian slums of the city centre. "Decanted", to use the horrible jargon of the housing bureaucracy. No one asked them if they wanted to go; public consultation was an idea whose time had not yet come. The people were dumped in a field – a former aerodrome, in fact – and left to rot. They rotted.

Most of the tenants of Castle Vale lived – existed would be a more appropriate word – in 34 high-rise blocks. No one warned them that these houses had been built using untried methods; or that they would become structurally unsound and severely damp; or that they would be difficult, as well as ruinously expensive, to heat. No one prepared them for the physical and psychological isolation of the estate, with its flat, characterless landscape and its acute claustrophobia. All this the people had to discover for themselves.

In 1983 – Mrs Thatcher was in power now – the BBC sent a film crew, including the novelist Beryl Bainbridge, to make a documentary series about what they saw and heard in the towns and villages of England. One of the places they visited was Castle Vale. Beryl Bainbridge wrote afterwards (in a book of the series) that the unemployed of the 1930s at least had a structure of home and chapel to support them; nothing then could have matched the degradation of being out of work and an inhabitant of Castle Vale.

Twelve years on, and poverty in Britain has been abolished. We have the Government's word for it. We have the *Daily Telegraph*'s word for it. And here I am, just off the bus from Birmingham, picking a hazardous route through broken glass and scavenging pigeons outside a shopping arcade. The gable end has been defaced by a British National Party slogan and a spray-painted message which declares that Clare is a slag. The arcade consists of: William Hill, bookmaker; boarded-up shop; boarded-up shop; Mrs Patel, grocer; Dillons, newsagent; Bill, butcher (closed); boarded-up shop; and, finally, a pub with a heavily ironic name: Trade Winds.

Precious little trade has ever blown this way. On the other side of the main road, a boundary as remote as the

Amazonian jungle, expensive cars are produced for people who used to be called rich but are now called independent. Meanwhile, people who used to be called poor but are now called dependent enjoy an excellent view of the Jaguar plant from the roofs of their crumbling tower blocks. It is the nearest any of them will come to a Jaguar or its production line.

"She says" – I have Beryl Bainbridge's book open – "that the police patrol in pairs, and the alsatian dogs run in packs."

"Artistic licence!", Tess Randles replies bravely. Miss Randles has one of the more unenviable jobs in the Midlands. She is public relations officer for Castle Vale.

A year ago, after the people voted in a referendum to dissolve their unsuccessful marriage to Birmingham City Council, the estate was acquired by a Housing Action Trust – one of six in various parts of the country – which has set itself the enormous task of rebuilding the ghetto and generating a viable local economy. Already it has invested £7 million of Government money; in the next decade it expects to spend a further £100 million.

"A holistic approach is the only answer," says Tess Randles. "It won't be enough to give people better housing. We need to improve work skills and deal with the health problems on the estate."

"How will you do that job any better than the council?"

"That's quite complicated. We have the advantage of being on site. And we believe in involving people. We ask them constantly how they want to see the estate develop. We encourage them to join committees. And when our job is finished, we hope the people who live here will decide how Castle Vale should be run."

At the heart of the new idealism, there remains an implicit and unanswered question about the failure of local democracy. It was the Town Hall which created this monstrous place, substituting as an act of public policy one slum for another, which cruelly neglected to deal with the consequences, and which finally acknowledged, at God knows what cost in broken lives, that it could no longer cope.

At any time in 26 years, it could have chosen to come closer to the people. It chose to stay remote.

The long bleak road through Castle Vale used to be a runway for a Vickers Armstrong aircraft factory. During the Second World War, it launched 12,000 spitfires. As a gesture of repentance for what was done to Birmingham in the name of a hard-won peace, they should have dropped a bomb on the high-rise blocks. Instead they are demolishing them slowly, as if to make quite sure. This morning, wintry sunshine pours through a gaping hole in the roof of Bovingdon Tower.

At the end of the road, in a semi-derelict square of shops, tapestries hang in the window of a laundry. Their mottoes mock the squalid surroundings. *There's No Place Like Home. All Things Bright and Beautiful.* "Lovely day!" a stall-holder greets me. He is selling dolls. A girl, who looks about 15, legs concentration-camp thin, carries a tiny baby in her arms with profound tenderness. From another of the stalls, a middle-aged man, bowed and worn, buys a second-hand album and a book. The book is by Dickens, the music by Beethoven. This man is among the poorest in Britain. He has 10p with which to exercise an intelligent choice. But, for a moment, he seems no more dependent than the editor of the *Daily Telegraph*, who, being human and civilised, will also derive spiritual solace from books and music.

After Castle Vale, I have begun to question the meaning of the word dependent. It is easier to define poverty. Poverty is unemployment of 26%, and 45% of 16-20 year-olds who have never worked. Poverty is no sixth form at the local comprehensive, and 54% who leave without qualifications. Poverty is 57% of households on incomes of less than £99 a week, and 22% whose health is so poor that their homes require physical adaptation. That is poverty. That is real. The rest is merely propaganda.

A little ooh-la-la

Leicester

You may be unaware that one of the curses of modern civilisation, the package tour, began in Leicester when Thomas Cook chartered a train to Loughborough. Surprisingly little has been heard of the Leicester holiday industry since that historic day in 1841, but recently there have been hints of a revival.

In the summer, the *Independent* advised its readers to "travel back to the Naughty Nineties, a time when champagne was the drink of choice, joie de vivre the watchword and liaisons were, as often as not, just a little dangereuses." This was the paper's way of promoting a "wicked weekend" at a country house hotel in Quorn, a few miles from the city. Peter Preston, former editor of the *Guardian*, who had the misfortune to be brought up in Quorn, wrote in the *Spectator* that he could think of better places for a wicked weekend and advised readers seeking a little ooh-la-la to try the Holiday Inn, Leicester.

They gave me room 401, overlooking the car park, for £59 excluding breakfast, excellent value considering that it entitled me to a bed, a trouser press, a bath for the vertically challenged, towel and soap, a mini-bar, and a drawer containing a hair dryer, an ashtray, and the Holy Bible. A few caveats are necessary. I gave up cigarettes years ago; I am terrified of mini-bars; I have yet to meet anyone who admits to having used a trouser press in a hotel room. But, short of actually pressing my trousers, getting stuck in the bath for the night, or reciting the Book of Leviticus, I discovered in room 401 most of the prerequisites for a little ooh-la-la.

The bed – now, there was a bed. At a pinch, it would have accommodated the Liberal Democratic conference. And the TV – it had its own in-house adult movie channel, a boon to the tired businessman at £5.95 a day (unlimited viewing). *Slick Honey*, in which "the private dick's sexual stamina is tested to its limit", promised a wickedness normally experienced only by *Independent* readers in Quorn. But here's another of those tedious caveats: ever since a press facility trip to Copenhagen in 1974, I have stuck to U-pictures.

Joie de vivre was the watchword for the reading material in room 401: a fixture list for the FA Carling Premiership, a copy of *Leicestershire Business Today* ("Exporting Can Be Fun!"), the Dawn to Dusk Information Up-Date with news of revised opening times at the Leicester Royal Infirmary History Museum, and an extensive menu for 24-hour room service. Among the listed dishes was Quorn Provencale, "pieces of Quorn served in a traditional provencale sauce, £12.25", which made me think nostalgically of wicked weekends almost beyond recall, when Peter Preston strolled down to the Quorn baptist chapel youth club for a game of ping-pong. Could I face pieces of Quorn? Friend, could you?

A leaflet apparently entitled Sex on Saturday turned out on closer inspection to be Sax on Saturday, and besides, this was Thursday. It has invariably been the fate of the executive traveller to be three days ahead of the action or three days behind it; when the original package tourists arrived in

Loughborough in 1841, you bet the brass band had just quit the district. But wait – here was the personal column of the *Leicester Mercury* advertising sauna massage in Lutterworth, a desert retreat in Loughborough, and an Egyptian whirlpool jacuzzi, plus Sky TV, opposite the St James Car Park. An Egyptian whirlpool jacuzzi sounds lovely; it's having to watch the Ryder Cup at the same time which is slightly daunting.

There were 22 in the cocktail bar before dinner, and every one a bloke. "Six hundred and seventy miles I've travelled today. And you know, I beat them down from £200 to £69. Return!" A new breed of bore is emerging, the Eurotunnel passenger regaling cocktail bars in Leicester with boastful tales of cutprice deals on Le Shuttle. But, just as some phoneys are genuine, so some bores are interesting. "You look a bit like Moshe Dayan tonight," he told one of his companions. Let's face it: it is not every day you hear someone being compared to Moshe Dayan, especially as poor Moshe died in 1981.

Dinner was served in the Hayloft restaurant. The architect had gone wild creating a theme of rural idyll, very East Midlands, with farmhouse chairs on their side as if the cowboys had just rolled in from Quorn, elderly suitcases out of an H.E. Bates serial, bales of hay. No one was even pretending to roll in the stuff, least of all the bulbous-eyed solitary businessmen scattered about the barn like so many startled pigs.

A poster advertised the Wyvern Laundry Tennis Club's private and select dance in the Abbey Cafe on 25 November, 1927, with Ken Hamilton and his Rhythm Aces Dance Band (buses arranged). Ah, those carefree days pre-Common Agricultural Policy, when liaisons in the Wyvern Laundry were, as often as not, just a little dangereuses! Tonight, in the absence of Ken and the lads, we had to make do with a drip-feed over the hotel speakers of some Radio 2 quartet in the early stages of anaesthesia.

At 8.39 I shook my watch, convinced that it had stopped. The shortage of ooh-la-la was so desperate that I resorted to abandoning the Holiday Inn for the rest of the evening and exploring the nightlife of Leicester. For a while, I stood on the grass verge of the Central Ring Road North, marvelling at the manic look of the motoring classes. When bells began to toll, I followed the sound until I came to its source. Above a gate a notice said: "Welcome to Leicester Cathedral". The gate was padlocked. There were vacant parking lots for the verger, the precentor, the chancellor, the master of music, the bishop. Verily, I say, there was even a lot for the archdeacon of Loughborough.

A few yards on, young people were spilling into discotheques. "If you've got any requests or dedications," yelled a DJ, "you can bugger off." A group of four – two boys, two girls – walked briskly towards a door guarded by Neanderthal chaps with evil scowls. "She goes like a train," one of the boys said. "You're disgoosting," a girl giggled in reply. "Well," said the boy, "men are." And happy, affluent, self-assured they looked, the youth of middle England on this balmy evening, fearing neither war nor God nor revolution, as the bells tolled in the padlocked cathedral and no one dreamt any longer of asking for whom.

By 11 o'clock, the bar of the Holiday Inn was deserted. All along the corridor, I could hear late-night television: Kirsty Wark, Kirsty Wark, what might have been the climax of *Slick Honey*, more Kirsty Wark. I am sorry to disappoint Peter Preston, but it does seem that, when you go to the Holiday Inn, Leicester, you get very little ooh-la-la and a shocking amount of Kirsty Wark.

Back in room 401, I slept soundly and awoke feeling unusually cheerful. Perhaps Leicester agrees with me. But next time, ooh-la-la will be unconfined. I will insist on taking Peter Preston for company.

The town that likes to say no

Oxford

Who or what is Crampton Hodnet? An absent-minded vicar, perhaps, who clings to the old Bible and opposes women priests; or a Cotswold village of honey-coloured cottages; or, just conceivably, a mild seizure of the leg muscles. Whatever he or it is or was, I went to Oxford with the intention of solving this literary detective mystery. Though no Morse, I rather fancy myself as a foot-slogging Sergeant Lewis.

There was only one lead: Barbara Pym wrote a novel of that name and you cannot get a copy of it for love or money. Booksellers, asked to account for the missing volume in the Pym collection, look up a microfiche and affect an air of surprise. "It's listed," they tell you, "but not currently available." Fat lot of good.

After years of frustration, I had begun to feel like poor Mr Hartley from the *Yellow Pages* commercial. But the prospect of a visit to Oxford offered fresh hope. If the elusive Hodnet was to be found anywhere, it would surely be in one of the many excellent bookshops of that scholarly place, especially since Miss Pym, a graduate of St Hilda's College, lived in the area and actually set her novel in Oxfordshire.

The entrance to Dillons was guarded by a crocodile of Japanese tourists. "What's up?", I asked their leader. She did not reply, but smiled in that inscrutable way which might have hinted at a delayed tour coach, a second Hiroshima, or some contingency of intermediate gravity. Half an hour later they were still there, patient as you like. Waiting for Crampton Hodnet, I shouldn't be a bit surprised.

Dillons had never heard of it, nor Blackwell's, and in an antiquarian bookshop the mere mention of the word "novel" reduced the temperature by several degrees. "We don't *do* modern fiction," the woman at the desk said icily. Hey, sorry for asking.

A few yards up the street, in another second-hand joint of superior pretension, the atmosphere was only slightly more congenial. Browsing is usually such fun, but in Oxford it is a case for the Crown Court. No Pym here either, needless to say, though I did come across a book entitled *Why Not Eat Insects?* This shop had a security monitor and the manager was looking closely at a white-haired old chap with a furtive manner. When it occurred to me that it was probably me, I left hurriedly.

"Mum's Lottery Nightmare", proclaimed a billboard for the evening paper, a surprisingly brash tabloid for such a brainy borough. *Ace Ventura* was on at the Odeon and *Mother Goose* at the Playhouse, as if the boring old bird should not have laid her egg by now. And in a 'phone box of the Randolph Hotel, a plaque declared that the Amateur Athletic Association was founded here in April 1880. I am not often cheered by the thought of people buying lottery tickets, going to rubbishy films, and holding meetings in 'phone boxes, but in Oxford one soon begins to long for vulgar humanity.

True, there are more vagrants and winos in the streets than

are normally encountered in England, even after 17 years of Conservative rule. I asked one young beggar how much she wanted. "Whatever you can afford," she replied mournfully. In exchange for 50p, she gave me a dirty look. Second year Eng Lit, no doubt.

And these are just the ones on the pavement. Heaven knows what dregs of humanity going by the name of Fellows lurk indoors.

A student publication concedes that many homeless people can be seen around the city, but reflects that "in this respect little has changed since the founding of the university eight centuries ago". The authors neglect the essential qualification that in 1215, when the university received its original charter, the establishment of the Welfare State was 730 years in the future, not 50 years in the past. The squalor of the streets mocks the claim of Oxford to produce the best brains in the country. It does not require much of a brain to create the clapped-out dump known as Great Britain.

Oxford has colleges as other towns have shops. The plate on which dinner was served in the Randolph Hotel bore the insignia of 27, most of which are rather too anxious to discourage public access. This is the town that likes to say "No". No Busking. Staff Only. Closed to Visitors. Private. Strictly No Entry. I think they are trying to tell us something. They are trying to tell us to push off.

At Balliol, two refugees from the vigil outside Dillons stepped tentatively beyond the gate. One produced a camera while the other posed. It was a tiny moment of innocent happiness which should have disturbed no one.

"That'll be £1," said a vigilant gauleiter known as a porter.

The tourists looked puzzled.

"Admission charge," he persisted. He was out of his box now. He was confronting the fare-dodgers.

It is difficult to resist a pang of patriotic shame when we behave so boorishly. The Japanese put their camera away and scarpered. But I paid the humiliating fee, which allowed me to stroll in the quadrangle. The languid sound of a saxophone drifted over the deserted gardens, and the stonework looked wonderfully serene. But the experience somehow failed to engage the emotions. It had been soured. No amount of glorious architecture could take away the bitter taste.

Perhaps the unfriendliest entrance in Oxford – this is to make a huge claim – is the one for the Bodleian Library. I stood there marvelling at a building so hostile to the encroachments of the outside world. Dare I enter and demand to see Crampton Hodnet? The Bodleian was sure to have it, for this is one of six libraries entitled by copyright law to a free copy of every book printed in the UK – "within one month after the publication" as the letter from the agent peremptorily puts it.

I did not dare.

But I did telephone the Bodleian afterwards to ask for guidance. Non-members of the university may request a reader's ticket for approved research, though only if supported by a letter of introduction.

"From whom?"

"Ah," they said. "Well, a professional person. Someone we can look up on a list."

With my letter of introduction and a cheque for £5 – £10 for a longer read – I must then appear in person and have my application *scrutinised*.

In my other life as a publisher, I have sent the Bodleian Library hundreds of free books and journals over the years. It is disappointing to learn that this generosity is not reciprocated and that for all practical purposes the library is open only to a privileged few. I may stop sending my publications as a protest, and risk imprisonment. But it would be nice to take Crampton Hodnet with me to the cells.

The 8.52 to Outer Mongolia

Slough

The 8.52am from Reading, which used to terminate at Slough, now goes all the way to Outer Mongolia. The railway company responsible for the revised timetable claims that a typist's error led to this unfortunate misprint, but it sounds to me like another bad joke at the expense of Britain's most reviled borough.

You may remember John Betjeman's extreme solution:

Come, friendly bombs, and fall on Slough
It isn't fit for humans now.

A native of Ohio, asked what he was doing in Cleveland, replied: "You gotta live somewhere". Despite its reputation, many choose to live in Slough: 106,000 at the latest count. Is it enough to reflect that these misplaced souls gotta live somewhere? Or – subversive thought – could it be that Slough is somewhat under-rated?

I discovered that it has many unsung merits, not the least

of which is that it isn't Oxford. After Oxford, Widnes would be fun.

Next among Slough's virtues, the weather sparkled all day long. Such well-loved local landmarks as the Brunel bus station and the underpass to the town centre were cast in a cheerful glow by a strong winter sun. The air felt light.

I plunged into the underpass pursued by two boys on bicycles. They said "excuse me" as they breezed past. Politeness among the young is rare enough to be worthy of remark. The underpass – I have become something of a connoisseur of the underpass – was clean and graffiti-free, denoting a civic pride by no means commonplace. At the end there were two further underpasses, one marked "Town", the other "University".

Slough, though not widely celebrated as a seat of higher learning, is the home of Thames Valley University. Here, students may specialise in essential food hygiene, potter with clay, avail themselves of a wide variety of midwifery modules, do an advanced certificate in marketing or, if they absolutely insist, learn how to write television scripts for the next generation of British sitcoms.

In the recreational block a poster advertised "heavy duty sauna", designed for guilt-ridden Presbyterians.

I wandered freely in the foyer and corridors, used the telephone, picked up leaflets, strolled into the gym, yet still no one uttered a word of objection. A very relaxed place, Thames Valley University. There was a modest amount of heterosexual kissing going on in public, a pretty daring activity these days, even by Slough standards.

A newspaper once reported that the town's main car park was listed among the local visitor attractions. Another of the tourist highlights – I am making this bit up – is the Slough of Despond public house. But I did find a pub called the Slug and Lettuce (bar lunches a speciality). It is not in the borough as such, however, but in the neighbouring suburb of Windsor.

In the High Street, one or two natives were watching television in shop windows. "Labour's spokesman for consumer affairs", a Mr Griffiths, who was being interviewed outside the Houses of Parliament, was wearing one of those Rotary Club suits that today's career socialists like to sport. He looked suitably grim and consumer affairish. The fact that you couldn't hear a word he said helped enormously.

Slough is old-fashioned enough to have policemen on the beat, pounding it in broad daylight. Better still, it has an exceptionally nice policewoman, WPC 237, who helps little old ladies across the street and smiles winningly at visitors. If you are ever arrested in Slough, may you be lucky enough to have WPC 237 as your escort.

It is a caring town. People queued in the street to sign a petition against scientific experiments on animals. I was so worried about what they do to cats that I gave £1. "Cheers," said the collector.

Literate, too. The newsagent stocked the *Economist*, *Private Eye*, *Prospect* (that's the new one with longer articles than the others), and *Bella*.

And you get a very good haircut in Slough, even if you are not up to a heavy-duty sauna.

"Any chance of an appointment?"

"In about 15 minutes, love. What's your name?"

"Roy."

"OK, then, Roy, we'll see you in 15."

When I returned to Elite Hair (formerly Top Cut), a woman was having her hair permed. "He's in a rut with his work, he's in a rut with me," she was confiding to the hairdresser. Hairdressers are the new priests. But the customer seemed quite cheerful about this Sloughish state of affairs. She said the answer to everything was Tai-Chi.

The one who cut my hair had rings in her nose and tattoos on her shoulders.

"Which county is this?"

"Berkshire," she replied with a giggle.

"What's so funny?"

"Well, I suppose people think of Berkshire as all leafy lanes. Not a bit like Slough."

"You don't like the town?"

"Oh, it's fine," she said warmly.

"Have you ever heard of the John Betjeman poem?"

"Yeah, my grandad keeps promising to give me the words."

I recited the relevant verse. She said she didn't mind its sentiments. Here, then, is another disarming characteristic of this admirable place: when Sir John Betjeman suggests a controlled nuclear explosion to rid the world of their town, the people take his idea in good part. They even manage to laugh.

As if I have not said quite enough in praise of Slough, it has an excellent reference library, so crowded with serious readers that I had to wait for a desk.

A scholarly account of the borough begins with the unpromising statement that in its long history Slough has not figured in any great national events. Yet it is not without distinction. In 1845, John Tawell, the Salt Hill murderer, became the first criminal to be caught by electric telegraph.

Tawell travelled to Slough in the garb of a Quaker with a bottle of cyanide in his pocket. He administered the poison to his discarded mistress, Sarah Hart, whereupon she let out a piercing scream which aroused the neighbours. Tawell fled and caught the evening train back to London.

Within minutes, a message giving a full description of the suspect was circulated from the Slough telegraph office to the police in London. Tawell, to his astonishment, was arrested on his arrival at Paddington station and thus became one of the first victims of new technology. He was tried at Aylesbury and hung from the upper window of the court house, the last person to die in that position.

The notoriety of the case had an odd side-effect: it made the Slough telegraph office a popular tourist attraction. "Them's the cords that hung John Tawell," awe-struck pilgrims were heard to utter as they pointed to its many posts and wires.

The moral of the story is that, if you must poison your discarded mistress, it is advisable not to do so while dressed as a Quaker in Slough.

The visitors' book

Gatwick Village

There is no immediately apparent reason why anyone should need to visit Kefallinia or Faro. Yet, such is the restless spirit of the age, an increasing number of English people go voluntarily to a village in West Sussex, allow themselves to be intimately frisked, buy vast quantities of cheap booze, and risk an unnecessary death in order to be transported 30,000 feet, or its horrible metric equivalent, above the ground. Can Kefallinia or Faro be worth such an ordeal?

By booking a cheap day return on the Gatwick Express train, it is possible to avoid the horrors of international air travel while experiencing the vicarious thrill of it all. The senior conductor – not that I have ever met a junior one – may give your ticket a second look, for there are still comparatively few people who set out for Gatwick with the intention of returning the same day. Tell the senior conductor, if he expresses surprise, that you wish to see the place which is, for so many pilgrims, the last sight of England. And quite a sight it is, too.

Yes, there *is* somewhere in West Sussex called Gatwick Village, though it is not the picture postcard image of an English village. There is neither cricket pitch nor Norman church, neither grungy kids outside the Spar shop nor Sunday afternoon bikers. You will salivate in vain for the froth of real ale in an oak-beamed pub. At Gatwick Airport they have refined the traditional ideal of English rural life by creating an indoor village, with round-the-clock security and regular flights for the relief of terminal boredom. Here, indeed, is the quintessential village for our times.

It has proper streets with banks, shops, restaurants of a sort, and what they call an amusement arcade, not that anything could be less amusing than an amusement arcade. Between the departure of the 11.50 to Kefallinia and the 12.10 to Minneapolis (Frankfurt's boarding at gate 19), three grown men identically dressed in shorts and trainers, with white socks which reached almost as far as their tubby football supporters' knees, were diverting themselves with "simulated rally driving" before boarding a lunchtime flight to somewhere unbearable.

The inhabitants of this village lead a transient existence. When they are not feeding slot machines they are leaving crossword puzzles unfinished, secreting the marijuana, reading the sports pages, dreaming of bronzed girls with big breasts, getting tight, sleeping it off. They sprawl, mouths gaping, across lounge seats of strobing colours, and you wonder what would rouse them short of a practical joke that they had just missed the last call for Las Palmas.

But, mostly, they eat. They feast on delicacies such as "BBQ chicken sandwiches and open pit barbecue sauce", served on cardboard plates with miniature plastic knives and forks, in an open-plan canteen only slightly smaller than the average Fleet Street newsroom. Here you will find Baskin Robbins and Millie's Cookies and the Great Steak and Potato Co, whose functionaries holler into microphones when orders are ready. "No 76", they cry, and an old, done man with a stick hobbles to the pick-up point.

The marketing industry brought forth this joke village of Gatwick, just as it revolutionised the British pub with that exhausted platter of cheese, pickles and curled-up lettuce known as the ploughman's lunch. The imitations are so ridiculous that they appear to be a deliberate mockery of the original. But they are parodies playing on a genuine popular sentiment which may go quite deep. We want to believe that there are still real villages out there, with real ploughmen down from the farms. We hold to a myth.

From a shop in Gatwick Village called Glorious Britain, you may buy a teapot in the shape of a village police station, with a smiling bobby and a notice advertising a reward for a lost dog; another teapot is designed as a village store and post office; another as a branch-line pre-Beeching railway station. The tea comes pouring from some forgotten autumn when the English went, not on bucketshop trips to Faro, but on foot through damp, fresh-fallen leaves to a village church which had a vicar, and a graveyard, and a tattered old Bible written in glorious prose.

Has all this travel made us happier? I spent some time studying the tearful faces at the international departure gate, the blown kisses of lovers left behind. I must have looked even more suspicious than usual, for a security man came up and demanded to know my business. "Some of us" – he pointed to the stern uniformed figures on the other side – "think you're checking up on our security operation."

When I assured him that I was merely observing the melancholy condition of the human race, his face visibly relaxed. "Ah, well," he said indulgently, "this is one of the most stressful places in the world."

"You mean they're afraid they're going to die?"

"Not that," he said. "It's more to do with what we're going to find on them. They're usually OK after a couple of drinks."

But I think the security man is wrong, or only partly right. Gatwick Village in all its hideous clamour and tawdriness disguises a certain human vulnerability. Either by looking for it quite hard or, as I did, stumbling on it by accident, you will find in an otherwise deserted corridor a plain inter-denominational chapel. In it, there are free copies of the *Catholic Herald*, a quiet place to sit and pray, and a visitors' book remarkable for its candour and occasional wit. Here are a few typical entries:

"When I fly, I hope not to die."

"Dear God, please get me to Majorca safely and back, so I can see my grandad, and please let Terry win his football match at the Arsenal."

"Please look after Marlena and Jim in Bosnia."

"God help me over the next four and most important days of my life."

"I'm not sure if there is One, but if there is, make it good for her."

Another asks: "How ya diddlin', God?" and imagines His reply: "I'm not diddlin' that great. I've been waitin' for a plane for over six hours. Think I'll just go and create a hurricane over Miami to relieve my frustration." I like this idea of the bored deity, driven to mischief by an interminable delay at Gatwick and a surfeit of Millie's cookies.

It's 1.30, and a flight from Munster has arrived with Miss Daisy Haines among the passengers. There is an urgent announcement: she is to go straight away to airport information. Oh, Miss Daisy Haines of the melodious name, who, with a sharp intake of breath and a flutter of anticipation, is even now hastening to a desk for that awful thing: a piece of unknowable news. But she is down, and safe, and will soon be home in England; and, from the chapel here in Gatwick Village, that feels not too bad a prospect.

Gatecrashing the party

Christmas in Liverpool

I had never been to a proper office party. Come to that, I had never been to an improper one, though it seems to amount to the same thing. I have worked for most of my life alone or in groups too small and anti-social to be party-going. But when I went to Liverpool, I thought it might be fun to attend an office party. Somebody else's.

But whose? I started at the Britannia Hotel because Beryl Bainbridge, who was an actress in this city many boozy intervals ago, wrote well of it. I even tried to stay there. "How may I help you?" intoned a voice in Reservations. She couldn't help me. There was no room at the inn: all 376 rooms were occupied. Pity help Mary and Joseph, who will need en-suite facilities and a baby listening service if they arrive in the city within the next few days.

In a basement, people were eating and listening, or not listening, to an execrable tape of carols adapted for the age of disbelief – Bing Crosbied, Radio Twoed, Sing Something Simpled, Eurovisioned, and otherwise pulped into blandness. The choristers sounded as if they might have been embalmed round about the time of Mr Heath's three-day week.

In another basement, pretty girls whose short dresses glittered in the dark were dancing to loud music. This was obviously a party of sorts, but the fact that the girls were so young and appeared to be dancing with each other put me off. Call it cowardice.

It was almost 8 in the evening yet the shops were open, the streets crowded. Opportunists in baseball caps and bold striped shirts had set up stalls to sell hot dogs and doughnuts. The sickly-sweet aroma, the vicious cold and the air of impromptu carnival – only the absence of unprovoked homicide reminded me that this was Church Street, Liverpool, not 42nd Street, Manhattan. Merseyside had also organised an old-fashioned industrial dispute to mobilise the Christmas shoppers. "Support your dockers," implored the pickets, burly men with big hands, as if in some curious way the people owned them. Which, in this city, could almost be true.

The snow turned at once to slush but failed to obliterate the scrawled appeal under a photograph of Susan Penhaligon, who would now be in the middle of Act I, from a man so desperate for female company that he had left his name and address on the wall of the Playhouse. Outside the theatre a mother produced a box-like parcel from a shopping bag. "This is our family game," she said excitedly to a friend. "We always have a family game." The Cratchits live, even in the Britain of post-nuclear relationships.

An earnest young man with a tape-recorder and a microphone asked me if he could have a word.

"What does Christmas mean to you?" he began.

"The birth of Jesus Christ," I said.

He looked mildly disconcerted.

"Ah. And is there, er, anything that mars Christmas for you?"

"The fact that it starts in October and ends in January."

"Funnily enough," said the young man, warming to his assignment, "we had Hank Marvin on the programme yesterday. He claimed that Jesus was born in October."

"That explains it, then," I said.

I asked him how many associated Christmas with religious belief. He said that he had interviewed 10 people, of whom one was avowedly Christian. He seemed to think this fairly encouraging.

In Mathew Street, a guitar-strumming youth sang Beatles numbers outside what was once the Cavern Club. Near by there is an unofficial wailing wall where pilgrims may write a message or draw a sketch in honour of the hottest act since the Boy Jesus. Some idiot had drawn a likeness of Jimmy Corkhill, a seedy character from the Liverpudlian soap opera, *Brookside*, in which Christmas is referred to as Crimbo. I never heard anyone in the streets use the word Crimbo.

The *Good Food Guide*, a modern bible not so well-written as the original, recommended only one restaurant in Liverpool, the Armadillo. It was empty when I arrived and almost empty when I left two hours later. From a table by the window I had a front-row-of-the-stalls view of Mathew Street. Stay long enough, the *Guide* says, and you may see an arrest out there. I didn't, but the temperature was probably too low for breaches of the peace.

While they cooked the food, I looked over some notes. "Put your work away," the waiter counselled half-seriously when he brought me the brandy. "You think I should?" "Sure. Even Andrew Carnegie had a day off."

I still hadn't found an office party, but I hadn't looked very hard. After a good dinner I walked through deserted streets of half-eaten doughnuts and discarded copies of the *Liverpool Echo* with its front-page offer of 10,000 free turkeys, to a hotel of spectacular dinginess near Lime Street station, and climbed stairs half-heartedly bedecked with tinsel. How gloomy commercial decoration invariably looks.

Then a tiny Christmas miracle: an office party at the top of the stairs. The disc jockey was a fat man with a beard. He glanced constantly at his watch as if he ought to be somewhere else. Strobing lights picked out the guests, cowed into silence by the din, sitting disconsolately at round tables. Occasionally the fat man called for volunteers to join him on a dais to participate in karaoke, an exercise in communal tone-deafness.

I was assimilated into the company without difficulty. People smiled at me in a vague, knowing way. "I'm an imposter," I finally admitted to the woman next to me. "Whose party is this?" She replied that they were people who took money off other people. Good God, the Revenue? No, a well-known chain of Merseyside bookmakers. I had not realised that I could pass so effortlessly for a turf accountant from Huyton.

The party was acutely disappointing in that it failed to live down to expectations. People sang badly but behaved well. The drinking was moderate and, so far as I could tell, nobody ran off with anybody else's girl. The DJ looked at his watch a final time and declared that it had been a pleasure. People drifted soundlessly into the freezing night.

Next day, I went to a better party. With five other paying customers, including a babe in arms, I crossed the Mersey on the last ferry of the afternoon and listened to a disembodied commentary about the city's maritime history, all nautical monks and pop stars and busy Whit Sundays long ago. It didn't mention the recent sacking of 300 dockers.

As we returned from Birkenhead, the fragile winter light faded. The boat turned sharply for home and there, illuminated on every floor, was the glorious Liver building, a waterfront spectacle of purest delight. I felt a shiver of pleasure and fell in love with Liverpool on the spot. The best parties are the ones that happen spontaneously.

God in Brompton Road

Christmas in Knightsbridge

about 10am, worshippers began to congregate at a temple in Knightsbridge, London. They peered in the windows and pushed unavailingly at the doors. Even when the word went round that the building would not open for an hour at least, they refused to leave. They formed queues at the many entrances, and waited with the endless patience of the English to pay homage to the god of all department stores.

For the second time that morning I walked past Harrods and down Brompton Road. I had been up and about the deserted streets before dawn, when the only other person above ground was a harassed Asian newsagent. He had not had time to assemble the broadsheets; I collected the *Observer* in bits, put it together myself, and continued my pilgrim's progress to the Oratory of St Philip Neri.

I was brought up as a Calvinist Scot; nominally I still am.

It was a faith that locked us into a church on the stroke of 11 – I mean, they actually bolted the doors behind us – and locked us out again at noon. To people of my background and disposition – well, at any rate, to me – one of the incidental allures of Catholicism is that, like the Asian corner shop, it is open all hours.

The doors of the Brompton Oratory are unlocked each morning at 6.30. While the world sleeps it is possible at that frail hour to pray or weep in decent seclusion. A woman knelt in one of the side chapels of the Oratory; an old man was bent in contemplation near the altar. There were no robed priests to tell us how it is or should be or will be. We were left to our own devices, and it was wonderful. It was a private heaven of soft light and shadow. You could have heard a pin drop.

This is not an old church; it is only a hundred years since its dome was completed to the design of the delightfully-named H. Gribble. But it has a particular quality of serenity. You might well long to return to it. Here is a story of someone who did.

In 1948, Mary Henderson was covering a guerrilla war in Greece for *Time* magazine. She drove to the front with an incongruous figure in a loud cap who mumbled constantly as their jeep dodged mine craters and disembowelled mules. "Konitza lies on the lap...on the slope...in the arms...pinned against..." Her companion was writing his piece.

To stop his mumbling, Mary Henderson asked him: "Where would you like to be at this moment if you could be transported there?"

"Entering the Brompton Oratory in my best Sunday clothes," Patrick O'Donovan replied without hesitation.

O'Donovan was an Irish Catholic whose forefathers came from a little town in West Cork called Clonakilty. All over the world, when Irishmen gathered and Clonakilty was mentioned, the words "God help us" were added. It was that sort of town. O'Donovan, however, was born in Richmond, Surrey, the son of a Harley Street specialist. He was a major in the Irish Guards during World War II and afterwards he became a great reporter.

His descriptive power, unknown now, was rare even then, but it was not his genius with words alone that made O'Donovan great. It was his essential humanity, his love of familiar places and ordinary people.

He did not often spend Christmas at home. He saw too much war and too many deaths. One Christmas he was in Bethlehem when Arabs shot at his car out of the darkness. "At midnight," he wrote, "the clangour of the bell, announcing again one piece of news that has never lost its savour, will rock across a country rent in two and constrained for the last time by British law. There will be little peace and no goodwill." Another Christmas he celebrated in a bleak railway carriage between Dusseldorf and Hamburg among the ruins of a defeated Germany.

He spent Christmas 1948 in revolutionary China, in a Jesuit mission house with its windows barred and its doors locked. He was preparing for sleep in an ice-cold room decorated with dark furniture and pictures of the saints when the bishop knocked at his door and asked him to serve midnight mass in the cathedral. There was a heap of bedding at the back of the church; a smell of poverty and unwashed wool rose above the incense and the wax. The Chinese "knelt in complete absorption" while shooting continued in the streets. A few months later the town was in Communist hands.

Patrick O'Donovan died at Christmas, 1981, aged 63. He lived long enough to see the decline of Christian belief, though not to report the more spectacular eclipse of Communism. Now, in the absence of those two competing saviours, it seems that all we have left are bewildered materialists outside a department store, not quite sure what they are doing or why. Yet some still celebrate the birth of Christ. Walk the extra mile. No, three hundred yards from Harrods will do. Go to Patrick's beloved Oratory.

For much of Sunday they celebrate mass every hour on the hour, separated by the briefest intervals. This non-stop observance manages somehow to be at once theatrical, dignified and relaxed, so that you may arrive without embarrassment in the middle of one service and leave in the middle of the next. You may choose to take no part in the sacrament, but sit alone at the side or light candles for the souls of the living and the dead. You may stand at the back as I and several others did. If you are very small you may even roll about in the aisle to your heart's content.

When I returned at 10.30, the Oratory was full. A voice said: "Take this, all of you, and drink of it. This is the cup of my blood." A queue longer than the one in Harrods' toy department stretched almost to the door.

"They knelt in complete absorption." The faithful were kneeling still: old men with sticks and battered homburgs; sexy red-haired girls in black leggings; elegant middle-aged women, dripping with fur and perfume, whispering Latin responses; the poor, cheaply anoraked and baggy jeaned; overcoated professional men clutching the *Sunday Telegraph*; a disturbed woman embracing a crucifix; young lovers holding hands; the dying who might not last five minutes.

"Do this in memory of Me." And, while police sirens wailed in the faithless streets, these people queued to drink the blood of Christ: hundreds of them, at mass after mass, in a ceaseless flow of humanity. Was this amazing spectacle the mere residue of Christian belief? Perhaps. Yet what an enduring and universal residue!

And I thought of the man from Clonakilty, God help us, the hero I never met, for whom Christmas represented "the gentlest and most lovely idea that mankind ever conceived, more beautiful than Aphrodite and her waves." I would have lit a candle for that splendid soul had courage not failed me. I expect he was there anyway, in his best Sunday clothes.

Market day

Diss

When he stepped from an express train on to a windy platform in Norfolk, John Betjeman was drawn at once to a pleasing pub called the Jolly Porter, the only watering hole between the station and the market town of Diss one mile away. He arrived at a disagreeable hour, i.e. before opening time. I followed in Sir John's footsteps, intending to propose a toast to that melancholy observer of vanishing England.

There was no evidence of the Jolly Porter, but they remembered it at the station. "Oh, it's been away for years," someone said. "The old woman who had it, she fell and broke her hip and it never re-opened." They demolished the pub and, in the true spirit of the new Britain, built a cement works on the site.

"A population of 4,000 which has neither grown nor shrunk over the centuries, an excellent service of trains to

Norwich and London, no main road through it to murder pedestrians and take the trade from the shops – in fact, the perfect small English town," noted Betjeman. He advised visitors to come on a Friday, market day. I took his advice and directed the taxi driver to drop me in Market Square.

There was indeed a market of sorts, though not of any peculiarity or distinction, with stalls selling fruit and veg, groceries and confectionery, trinkets, second-hand books and videos, cheap clothes. "Give yourself a treat, suck on a sweet," implored a latter-day Betjeman. On a kindlier morning the patter merchant might have attracted customers, but on this vicious Friday there were few takers for Tilley's rhubarb custards and sherbet lemons. It was not a day for staying sweet. It was a day for staying alive.

Mr Blowers, the Michael Fish of East Anglia, had warned us what to expect, yet I came ill-prepared for Diss on its coldest day of the decade, wearing lighter clothes more suited to winter north of the border. But, in Market Square, an entrepreneur saved my life. He was the only man in town with a big broad smile.

"Three pairs of thermal socks," I begged, "and a woolly hat before it's too late, and name your price."

"£4.98 for the lot," he replied. Done.

I changed into this Arctic gear on the spot – or rather on a bench thoughtfully provided by Mr and Mrs Belton of the Card Shop – and made straight for another pub recommended by Betjeman. Unlike the Jolly Porter, the Greyhound has survived the late 20th-century zeal for comprehensive redevelopment. It is one of those splendid English boozers with a well-tended log fire – before which I thawed-out with a double whisky and a plate of home-made vegetable soup.

Its ruddy-faced regulars in their Barbour jackets talked with glorious contempt of London, as if it were some distant planet. "It says in the London papers...", one man addressed his companion, meaning: "You can't believe a word you read in them". He discarded the metropolitan broadsheet rag and turned with relief to the *East Anglian Daily Times*, as I would myself if I lived there.

Yet, though the Greyhound was warm and civilised, it failed to rumble with the talk of farmers as it did for Betjeman. And the (Greek Revival) Corn Hall next door, formerly an animated place of banter and barter on market day, was closed. Bunting across its entrance gave notice of a Cajun Ceilidh in aid of Greenpeace, the nearest thing to a forthcoming attraction.

Down Norfolk roads, to the noisy saleyards of Diss, once flowed streams of pigs, cattle, goats, donkeys, ferrets, rabbits, and poultry. It was like this in the early 1700s when Daniel Defoe listed Diss among the principal market towns of the area; it was still like this two and a half centuries later when Betjeman came with a camera and a keen eye. Yet so completely has the recent past been dislocated from all that went before, few in the streets could remember when Diss ceased for all practical purposes to be a proper market town in the old, grand sense. The grave of the agrarian culture is strangely unmarked.

One of the local auction houses sold up. Another, Thos. Wm. Gaze & Son, continues the tradition on a diminished scale with regular sales of furniture, timber, eggs, and small livestock. When I arrived near lunchtime, the auctioneer was flogging rolls of wire netting for £7 apiece "to the lady on my shoulder" or to anyone else who felt an urgent requirement for a roll of wire netting. Such a changed scene may be delightful to a vegetarian, but it is simply not Diss.

"Because it is self-contained, friendly and contented, it is naturally threatened with overspill on the edges," Betjeman wrote. Those were prophetic words. In the 1960s, when the bogus idea of endless economic progress was widely believed, Norfolk County Council proposed the creation of a new town in Diss with a population of 100,000. Of course, it was perfectly crazy, yet the plan was opposed locally by the merest whisker of the chairman's casting vote. "We must live in the future," said one councillor, "or we shall fail future generations."

The new town went elsewhere; Diss failed future

generations with admirable equanimity. But what happens to a town when it no longer has any particular reason for existing? This question is often asked of the brutal industrial cities of the north, but it is just as true of much of rural England. You can tell if the rot has set in by the quality and diversity of the shops in the high street. Diss, which used to be reputed as a place of ironmongers, has become a place of charity shops.

"Bobby's?" repeated a middle-aged woman when I mentioned the name. "Never heard of it." Yet this was a local institution, a draper's with classic Victorian fittings which so delighted John Betjeman that he recommended a visit.

An older woman in the library looked thoughtful. "Goodness," she said, "Bobby's must have closed 10 years ago at least. I think it's an optician's now."

"How sad."

"Well, yes, we're quite a dead little town these days."

It had started to snow. "I do believe it's settling," they said in the shops. It fell on incongruous stalls of Mediterranean fruit and frilly knickers. "Half the stall-holders haven't bothered to show up," a man said. "Can't say I blame them." Down by the mere, it fell on quacking ducks and up by the station on the ghost of the Jolly Porter. It fell, too, on Mount Street, "one of the pleasantest country town streets left in England" according to Betjeman, who marvelled at its colourful mixture of brick and plaster, garden and park.

And in Mount Street it fell on the local headquarters of the Child Support Agency and on the claimants' letterbox of the DSS.

Eddy's

Spennymoor

Once, in the Laing Art Gallery, Newcastle upon Tyne, I saw a painting which haunted me for years afterwards. It was a street scene of an anonymous northern town, a mining town perhaps, on a wet night in deep winter. Opposite a long, unbroken row of decently small houses stood a corner shop, a fish and chip shop, warmly lit and inviting.

Despite the weather there were people in the streets – the customers. They looked poor but respectable; not special in any way. Yet the whole scene was animated by such a sense of belonging, of community, that I wanted to disappear into the painting and join the queue for a Saturday night fish supper. Salt and vinegar? Yes, please. Any pickles?

The picture seemed so realistic in every detail that I decided art should meet life: one day I would seek out that fish and chip shop, savour its aroma, have my bag wrapped in some redundant newspaper, walk out into the dark, hurry home in the rain.

Finally having an excuse to fulfil this ambition, I called the Laing and established that the shop was known as Eddy's. Where could I find it? No one at the gallery had a clue, but they did give me the name and address of a man who would know. So, in search of the elusive Eddy, I travelled south from Newcastle into the coal-mining heart of County Durham.

They do not have pits here any more. They have Thorn EMI. They have Electrolux. They even have Tony Blair for an MP. But they also have a much more important local celebrity: the painter of Eddy's.

"You'll stay for lunch," Norman Cornish said. "Or you might call it dinner. I knew a man who called it dinner until he bought a car. After that he called it lunch."

I am a non-motorist: we settled for dinner at noon.

Norman lives in Spennymoor, the pit town where he was born 76 years ago. The son of a miner, he left school in the depths of the 1930s Depression. The local colliery, the Dean and Chapter, where he started work, was nicknamed the butcher's shop in grim acknowledgement of its safety record. "You've just signed your death warrant, son," the colliery manager cheerfully informed him. He was 14.

He became a hewer of coal. At the end of the week, the miners were rewarded for their united production by a lump sum which they divided among themselves. He remembers the humiliating weekly spectacle of men down the pit trying to work out what each was due. Their oil-lamps were held low as they carefully placed the money in a newspaper on the ground so as to avoid losing precious coins in the dust.

Such experiences would have turned many sensitive men into political agitators. They turned this one into an artist. He had always possessed a natural ability – on his first day at school he won a prize for his drawing of a boot – but few God-given talents blossomed in an industrial society of harsh, circumscribed lives. For Norman Cornish, ability was happily married to chance: he discovered the existence of a sketch club. Entering that place of light and hope, he says, was like stumbling on wonderland.

He used his immediate surroundings as raw material, recording the way of life of the miner and his family. In time he was recognised by the art world and earned a reputation as the pitman painter. He despises the label. "It implies that there is something extraordinary about a miner who paints," he says. "Why shouldn't a miner paint?"

He never took a sketchbook to work. He was always too busy working. Instead he took it to the miners' pubs, where he executed quick character studies of the men he knew. "They were broad-minded fellows. I think they quite enjoyed it. I don't think they even noticed me. I was just a piece of furniture. Well, I was one of them. I liked those people because they were being themselves. They weren't pretending. And people sometimes sit in such lovely attitudes, don't they?"

As he gained experience, his art deepened into a vision of man's destiny on earth. "Spennymoor didn't have any cathedrals. The people themselves were the cathedrals. Early one morning I was plodding to work and watching this fellow in front of me. It was raining. A drop of rain hit my eye and there was a sort of explosion. Those telegraph poles bunched together – suddenly they looked like the crosses on Calvary."

He began to see the people and things around him in a different way. Miners could be glow-worms or angels in the sky; the chimney pots were little men turned upside down; the paving stones reminded him of piano keys – for painting, not playing. Washings on the lines were dancers in the wind. The shape of two men deep in conversation suggested a bridge. His wife Sarah knitting evoked a figure at prayer.

Without stepping out of Spennymoor, he created a metaphysical universe – "everything knitted into the same woolly jumper". He lived to see the jumper fall apart at the seams.

"The thing I remember and miss most is the lovely companionship of the miners. Sometimes we used to have hellish rows, but even that was companionship. It was a kind of massive symphony. I hope what I've done in my painting is to show what it was like to be alive in my lifetime, to have got those things down before they vanished forever."

Dinner was over. Still we hadn't talked about Eddy's. When I raised the subject, Norman said that it wasn't the shop which had interested him. He had been excited by the shape of the picture, the artistic possibilities.

"Still, tell me about Eddy."

"They were a well-known local family. O. Eddy – that was the name above the shop in Craddock Street – stood for Ossy, though I seem to remember it was Stan Eddy who ran the place."

"Is it still there?"

"Not for years. There's a car park on the site."

Norman showed me a photograph of the shop. The warmth and continental vitality of that hinted-at interior in the painting had been a work of the imagination – a flash of incongruous magic. In reality Eddy's had been nothing more than a drab chippy on a corner, just as the Jolly Porter had been nothing more than a railway station bar run by a strange old woman.

But *a car park*? By the time I got to Diss they had demolished the Jolly Porter and built a cement works in its place. I didn't have a drink in the Jolly Porter; I wasn't having a fish supper in Eddy's.

A philosophical city

Newcastle upon Tyne

At the end of that memorable television series, *Our Friends in the North*, Geordie had just escaped from prison, Nicky was mourning not only the loss of his mother but the death of his ideals, and Mary had suffered the unhappiest fate of all: she had become a rising star of New Labour. Indeed the only member of the original quartet with something to smile about after 30 years was the resourceful Tosker, an unreconstructed child of Thatcherism, happily re-married with kids and proud owner of a floating nightclub in Newcastle. The others thought they could change the world. They didn't.

Some admirers of the programme have criticised the rejection of political idealism in the final episode, the implication that society at large can no longer be reformed, the emphasis on personal satisfaction as a panacea. But wait – isn't that exactly how it is? We may not have liked it, it certainly wasn't a pretty sight, but the denouement of the series felt suspiciously like a snapshot of modern Britain. Put not your trust in Tony Blair. Put it in Tosker.

Friday night in Newcastle convinced me that a cloakroom ticket for a floating nightclub rather than a membership card for the Labour Party more accurately reflects the spirit of the age. Tosker's former wife, Mary, may be doomed to a front-bench job in the Labour Government, but I doubt if most people in Geordieland seriously care what the Labour government does or, more likely, does not do. The popular thing, the only thing that matters, is to have a really good time. Eat, drink and be merry, for tomorrow we shall not die: we shall awake with a crashing hangover to find that nothing much has changed.

I spent Friday night in a pub called Sergeant Pepper and was lucky not to be smothered by waves of humanity – the convivial city in its party frock or smart suit. The music belonged to the day before yesterday, when people still half-believed that politics made a difference to their lives. Its ear-splitting volume rendered conversation impossible, but no one seemed to mind. The men – ear-ringed, bulky, crop-haired, quite a terrifying bunch – drank pint after pint of foaming ale and sullenly observed the passing scene. One could imagine them as bouncers at Tosker's new club.

Meanwhile, the women were left to dance with each other. They mimed to the cheap music, using their hands and especially their eyes to express the emotion of the songs. They might have been Sergeant Pepper's lonely hearts. "Bobby's Girl," they trilled. "I wanna be Bobby's Girl." But where was Bobby? Boozing his boxer shorts off.

One of the agreeable features of Newcastle on a Friday night is that women over the age of 30 refuse to feel excluded. They consider themselves proper ravers even as they approach the horrors of the bus pass. My companion, anxious to please, asked one of these women where we should go when the pubs shut. Evidently, at the stroke of 11, everyone piles into clubs. My companion explained that, as I was pushing it in years, I would prefer a quiet, relatively civilised club, if that wasn't too much of a contradiction in terms. Could she recommend one?

"Greys," she replied.

I rather liked the sound of Greys. I imagined that it might be one of Tosker's spin-off ventures, a last resort if the floating nightclub crashed against the rocks one stormy weekend. But I did not go to Greys. Instead I went boringly to bed in the Royal Station Hotel, a smashing old place of grand chandeliers, endless gloomy corridors and antique coat-hangers left over from the glory days of British Transport Hotels, before those graceful establishments were sold off to the private sector along with the rest of the family silver.

In the morning I walked a few yards round the corner to the headquarters of the Literary and Philosophical Society of Newcastle upon Tyne, a posh name for a splendid body. At the top of the stairs they have erected a statue in memory of James Losh, former Recorder of the city. His long testimonial begins: "Zealous in promoting the moral and intellectual improvement of mankind, he was one of the earliest patrons of this institution. Distinguished in private society for the gentleness of his manners and the kindness of his heart, in public for the consistency and firmness of his political principles, the course of his life was equally marked by benevolence and integrity..." Now, that's what I call an epitaph.

The Lit and Phil, as it is known locally, is 203 years old. It was the product of an age of inquiry, when intelligent people were excited by ideas and restless to extend the frontiers of knowledge. At a time when the classics and mathematics still provided the basis for most higher education, the society's founders organised regular courses of lectures in the essential but neglected sciences.

In the rooms of the Lit and Phil, George Stephenson first demonstrated the miners' safety lamp; Hugh Lee Pattinson described the process he had invented for separating lead and silver; William George Armstrong explained the principle of his hydraulic power machine; Joseph Wilson

Swan displayed his incandescent electric lamp. With its superb library, its laboratory facilities and its museum, the society provided the practical means for advanced research. It was a university in all but name – and eventually its example and inspiration, to say nothing of years of dogged campaigning by its leaders, led to the establishment of a college of science in the city.

Its pioneering days are over, but the society remains a useful and much-loved Newcastle institution. After Friday night at Sergeant Pepper, I recommend Saturday morning in the Silence Room of the Lit and Phil. The *Silence* Room. Oh, bliss! Here a clubber with a hangover may peruse *Enthusiasms of Methodists and Papists*, *Sixty Eight Years on the Stage* by Mrs Charles Calvert, or *The History of Hertfordshire* (Vol II). The room is guarded by a portrait of Trotter Brockett (1786-1842), who was only seven when the society was founded. He sounds like something out of Thomas Hardy. In fact he was just another of those amazing Tyneside philosophers.

It is a rare place for a brood as well as a read, this Silence Room. It is a place in which to ponder the fate of all the Newcastles, the great English cities which were once so zealous in their pursuit of learning, so fiercely independent of the metropolis, so keen to experiment, so receptive to new ideas. Whatever happened to that intellectual crusade in the provinces? To some extent it has been formalised in centres of higher education. To a large extent, however, it has disappeared. We have replaced our thirst for knowledge with a thirst for Newcastle Brown Ale and a place in footballing Europe. The future belongs to Tosker. The rest is silence.

Literally so, in the case of my Observer career. As everyone had been predicting for months, the editor was finally fired. I sent a fax to the "executive" who had dealt with my copy to say that I would be writing no more. He did not reply. I never heard from the paper again.

Bigger pieces of Scotland

Preface to Part II

I didn't go to Scotland much for the *Observer*, nor Wales for that matter, though I did have the good fortune (from a purely journalistic point of view) to be in Belfast on the day the IRA bombed Canary Wharf and the ceasefire broke down.

Small pieces of England seemed the right size for a detached observer feeling his way, but larger boulders were required to deal adequately with how this native felt about Scotland. That was partly if not largely the motive for starting the *Scottish Review* in January 1995: to give me and others the space to write at length about aspects of modern Scotland.

The magazine's circulation is fairly small – we have neither the time nor the resources to market it properly – but our faithful supporters subscribe year after year and keep it going as a small independent title in the teeth of the Scottish media monopolies. Three of the pieces which follow appeared first in early issues of the *Review* and were subsequently reprinted, in full or in part, by the *Scotsman*. The meditation on Linwood was commissioned by the *Scotsman* and appeared only in that paper.

The first of the quartet is an account of the Hanger 13 inquiry into the drug-related deaths of three young men in the west of Scotland. For me this was educational as well as disturbing. It taught me a great deal about young Scotland that I had only dimly perceived before; and it deepened my distaste for the popular literary culture of Irvine Welsh and his cronies. The second, set in high summer, is a diary of a mis-spent week filming for the BBC and the hidden comic agenda behind the making of the programme. The third journey – to Linwood – became in my mind as emblematic of a lost Scotland as Hanger 13, though for different reasons. Finally I took a walk along Princes Street until I found myself walking into the Scotland of my vanished youth, and could walk no further.

K.R.

Sweet bird of youth

The Hanger 13 inquiry

After the recent deaths and uproar about E [ecstasy] and how shit it is compared to what it used to be, I feel obliged to say that my friends and I will go on taking it every weekend just like we have done for the past four years...I love the buzz and I think the only way I'll stop is if I drop.
– G. Brown and the Perth Posse, in a letter to *M8*, a magazine for Scottish clubgoers

On 15 February 1995, Neil Gow, QC, Sheriff of Ayr, gave a judicial determination at the end of a six-day fatal accident inquiry. He found that John Nisbet, 19, and Andrew Dick, 19, died on 1 May 1994 and Andrew Stoddart, 20, died on 21 August 1994, in Ayr Hospital, all three deaths resulting from consumption of the drug ecstasy in the Pavilion, Ayr, also known as Hanger 13, at a public musical entertainment generally known as a rave. Sheriff

Gow said that ecstasy, a class "A" drug in the same category as heroin or cocaine, had no therapeutic or medical value. What follows is a day-by-day account of the hearing at Ayr Sheriff Court.

Week 1: Monday

> *We were present the night John Nisbet and Andrew*
> *Dick died. It was a great night and the place was*
> *bouncin', but it was far too busy and there was hardly*
> *any ventilation, so it felt like you were dancing in a*
> *sauna instead of a rave club.*
> – Hanger Posse, Ayr, in a letter to *M8* magazine

The inquiry has been allocated a bright room which almost succeeds in being cheerful. The press have been invited to fill the jury benches, but this lot don't look a bit like a typical jury. For one thing, there isn't a woman among them. Were reporters always so intimidating or is this a new breed to frighten the children? I lurk in the public benches behind a trio of burly geezers with cropped hair. They, too, might be reporters – or night-club bouncers.

The dock is empty. For the next week, the wife-beaters and the house-breakers will be punished in another place. Here in court 2, no one is on trial, no one is guilty, no one is going to prison. The purpose is to determine how three young men died and whether their deaths could have been prevented. It is nothing more than that, but it should be nothing less.

"Court will stand!"

A small figure, gowned and wigged, strides to the most comfortable chair in the room. "This is an important case which may raise matters of wide public interest," Sheriff Gow begins. At the end of a brief prepared text, he says he will repeat his statement for any television crews which "may be present" outside Hanger 13 prior to his inspection of the premises at 2.15. And so a media agenda is established from the outset. We are to be co-operated with – "used" in the nicest possible way. We ought to be a little uneasy. Maybe we're not.

The procurator fiscal, who has been instructed by the Crown to present the evidence, rejoices in the name James Kelman. A solicitor, James Reid, represents the management of Hanger 13. The only surprise in the group of interested parties under Sheriff Gow's bench is the presence of a layman, Jack Drummond, as spokesman for the Stoddart family. He tells the court he was Andrew's uncle.

It is 169 days since the death of Andrew Stoddart; he would have been 21 on Christmas Day 1994. It is even longer – 281 days – since the deaths of John Nisbet and Andrew Dick. They must have passed this building the night they died, for Sheriff Gow's courthouse is only a few strides from the seaside pavilion where boys scarcely old enough to be called men meet girls, dance, and pop pills. And now, at last, we are to hear what happened. Vital witnesses have been summoned. Many have been given immunity from prosecution.

Jean Nisbet, 41, New Cumnock

She agrees that John Nisbet, her son, was born and educated locally and that he was unemployed at the time of his death. How briskly the fiscal ticks off this inventory of one brief life: the task is accomplished in under 30 seconds.

On Saturday 30 April, he went to Hanger 13. Early on Sunday – about four in the morning – the police came to her door and told her to contact Ayr Hospital. She didn't have a phone in the house, so they took her to the police station. The hospital advised her to go to John's bed straight away.

"Had you any indication he was taking drugs?"

"I never saw any difference in John. Happy go lucky John. Never complained about anything."

He died at 11.30am on Sunday 1 May.

Andrew Stoddart, 45, Rigside, near Lanark

Andrew Stoddart's dad confirms that his son was a van driver and a member of Douglas Water amateur football team.

"You were aware that on Saturday 20 August last year he attended Hanger 13 in Ayr?" Yes: Andrew had been several times before.

"Were you aware that he had taken pills on any previous occasion?"

"Absolutely not."

"Andrew took ill that evening?"

"The police contacted us at half past one in the morning to say he had died."

Mr Stoddart joins his brother-in-law at the table. He remains there for the rest of the hearing, whispering an occasional confidence but more often withdrawn, a careful listener, head slightly bowed, the archetypal Scot of few words who understands that it is improper to show emotion in public. As the days pass, his silent fortitude becomes a kind of testament in itself.

Gillian, 20, unemployed, New Cumnock

The first of the Hanger 13 clubbers. The court has difficulty knowing how to label them. Sheriff Gow talks mostly about "young persons" or "patrons", the latter term evocative of Cliff Richard records in echoing halls of old wood with a faded sign at the door asserting the management's right to refuse admission.

By the end of tomorrow, Hanger 13's "patrons" will have dissolved into blue-jeaned, monosyllabic impersonality, but because this is the standard-bearer, I can picture her still. She is tall and her features are too sturdy to be pretty; she exudes a certain raw physical confidence. It is possible to imagine this girl around 6.30 on a Saturday evening, the deadly hour of custard pie television, when the streets of sour, derelict Scottish towns are at their emptiest and the old, sunk in lethargy, check their pools coupons. She is looking at herself in a mirror. She is getting the hell out of this.

Kelman puts a lot of leading questions very quickly. She answers "aye" to most of them. Aye, she'd known John Nisbet well. Aye, they'd gone regularly to Hanger 13. Aye, everybody was searched at the door. Aye, she'd taken a pill that night. Ecstasy. Had it any special markings? Aye, it had the markings of a dove. A wee white dove. And in the jury box, biros without tops scratch into shorthand notebooks this artless expression of devastating irony.

"What effect does it have?"

"It makes you feel good," the girl replies. "It makes you feel happy."

Sheriff Gow glances up from his notes. "Had you taken any alcohol that night?" It is his first intervention, and the reply appears to astonish him. "Aye," she says, "a bottle of Buckfast." "What, a whole bottle?" "Aye." She'd drunk it on the bus to Ayr.

John Nisbet, who didn't drink on the bus but took one and a half pills inside the hall, became ill and was removed outside by two bouncers. He was shaking. He couldn't talk.

"Later you found out he'd died?"

"Hmm."

She brushes past me on the way out, and I notice her nose is pierced by a tiny ring.

Brian, 20, slater, New Cumnock

Another of John Nisbet's pals explains how it works at Hanger 13. If you want stuff, you tend to buy as a group, each member contributing his share – a "whip-round" Sheriff Gow calls it in his jaunty way, bringing to mind a retirement collection for some long-serving sheriff clerk. Someone is delegated to approach a dealer. The price? Around £13 a pill. That night, the go-between returns with nine Es – about £120 of business in a single transaction.

Brian swallows one pill, another an hour later. They make you want to dance, so you become hotter and hotter, so then you buy a bottle of water at the bar – that's £1 a shot – and once you've drunk the lot you take your plastic bottle to the Gents and fill up from the tap, and that keeps you going for the night.

John Nisbet, who was wearing a fluorescent orange jacket, a baseball cap, and joggers under his trousers, had been warned by friends that, if he insisted on all that clobber, he wouldn't be able to stand the heat. Later in the evening, John wasn't saying much. He was just sitting there with his legs crossed, quite close to death, while the band played and sweat poured off young limbs.

Brian is followed by Tom, a factory worker, and Victoria, who isn't working at the moment, and Campbell, who isn't working at the moment, and Gary, who's just unemployed. Then there's James, 18, a draughtsman, who wears a tie for his morning in court and who, on the night John Nisbet died, took speed. He doesn't seem sure what speed is, but he knows it's different from ecstasy. Well, he's tried ecstasy too, but not that night.

"Speed gives you the feel-good factor?", Sheriff Gow suggests helpfully.

"Should do," the witness replies. Anyway, it's cheaper – eight quid a powder.

Stewart, 24, architectural technician, Cumnock

This one lives on a farm. He is different from the others. He has the bespectacled assurance of a junior bank official. He might be something voluntary in a Young Farmers' Club. And he goes to Hanger 13 by private car.

Were you approached that night? – Yes. *By whom?* – Don't know. A stranger. *Where was he?* – Parking his car across the road. *What did he say to you?* – He asked me if I'd like to buy some ecstasy. *Did you buy any?* – Not at that time. *But there was an arrangement to see him inside?* – There was. *Did you notice how many pills this man had?* – There was a girl in the car. She had a plastic bag full of something or other.

Alan, 21, apprentice, Prestwick

He approached a man in a corridor next to the toilets. Sheriff: "How did you know you might get drugs from him?" Witness: "Dunno. He seemed to be that kind of person."

Alan, 23, computer operator, Irvine

The show-off of the morning: he talks in a racy clubber's shorthand, refers to ecstasy as eccies, and claims to have downed four in one night at Hanger 13. The sheriff asks what the drugs do for him. "They make you pure full of it...they make you mad with it." James Reid, for the management, wonders if a Saturday night would be complete without ecstasy. No, Alan says, it would be dead boring.

Afterwards, the witness swaggers to the public benches.

He's stinking of after-shave. "Fucking brilliant," he whispers to a friend. On the steps outside, he is filmed by the television cameras. Tomorrow he will be all over the papers.

Clare, 20, student, Paisley

A boy she met in Hanger 13 gave her half an E. She had convulsions, collapsed, and ended up in Ayr Hospital. This morning she's wearing stylish gear that might have been inspired by the fashion mag under her arm. After this slender young thing come two more students – Ross, 18, and Gordon, 18, each of whom admits to having bought a gram of speed. "You just ask about," Gordon says, "and find out who's got the stuff." Child's play, it seems.

Suddenly, it's time for lunch.

"Great PR, it really is." In an Ayr restaurant, one businessman is boasting to another of his latest wheeze – giving away the car of the year as a prize. "Got it at a nice discount." Then the clincher: "Got a spot on West Sound." At another table, they're discussing League reconstruction. "Grassroots level...take some pressure off...too competitive...kids play the game naturally...well, we'll not solve it overnight..."

As the conversation drifts across the bistro, I try to visualise this secure little world in which kids play the game naturally before aspiring to own the car of the year. And then I walk back into the square, the scaffolded pile of the County Buildings flanked by two terraces of Georgian facades behind which premiums are paid, books balanced. At the far end there is the County Hotel; and, on the other side, about as far as you can get to the sea without falling in, there's the tower of the Pavilion with its collective memory of amorous Saturday nights.

But facades can be deceptive: this secure little world is not what it was. There may be a County Hotel and a County Buildings, but county there isn't. That ceased to exist in 1975, long enough ago to encompass John Nisbet's entire life. The seat of the former Ayr County Council accommodates, in addition to Sheriff Gow's court, a sub-regional office of a larger local authority which is itself about to disappear. The

Pavilion is no longer the old-fashioned dance hall in which nothing more lethal than heavy petting ever occurred. And along the prom, rosy-cheeked young men from the backwoods race fast cars – perhaps even the car of the year – at life-threatening speed.

After lunch, Sheriff Gow goes for a look-see. "He needs a haircut," a court officer mutters. One journalist records later that the sheriff during his famous procession to Hanger 13 is belted with golden watchchains and stiff with Jermyn Street pomp. All I manage to note is the bowler hat, which triumphantly stays on its owner's head, even in the teeth of a bone-chilling breeze.

What is the point of this exercise? If the sheriff felt it would be useful to see inside Hanger 13, he should have gone at 10 o'clock on a Saturday night.

While Neil Gow delivers to camera an alfresco reprise of his opening statement – "a highly unusual move", the BBC's representative notes with a hint of reproof – I attempt a breach of Hanger 13's security by marching into the foyer of the Piv. I am confronted at the door by an official in a teddy boy suit.

Unlike the weekend punters, I am not frisked for powders, pills, notebooks, or other offensive weapons. The teddy boy politely asks me to leave. I plead hypothermia; he relents. Mrs Ridha, the owner of Hanger 13, says she remembers me from somewhere. We chat in general terms about the case. "One verbally inadequate kid after another," I mutter. This turns out to be a tactless remark. She says sharply that patrons of Hanger 13, far from being verbally inadequate, are on the whole extremely bright. "Well, I suppose they're nervous," I add in a conciliatory tone. "Not half as nervous as I'll be when I give evidence," she replies.

The lawyers arrive for their private tour of inspection; the teddy boy shows me the door. I turn towards the prom and there at the side of Hanger 13 is a wooden hut bearing the words "Lost Children". Metaphors come too easily.

❖❖❖

Tuesday

Police were last night awaiting the results of tests on a
23-year-old clubgoer who collapsed and died on a dance floor
after taking ecstasy. John Robjent is the second to have died
at the Mirage nightclub in Windsor, Berkshire, in five
months after taking the drug.
– Report in today's *Guardian* (7 February 1995)

Most of the newspapers carry pictures of the bowler-hatted
sheriff with his silver-topped cane on the steps of Hanger 13
– a scene brilliantly evoked by Bella Bathurst in the *Scotsman*
as "Edwardianism meets ecstasy, lawful judgement in all its
sober quaintness meets fast and strobe-lit death". But the
Guardian has the most compelling photograph. Murdo
Macleod's shot of a group of Ayr ravers "dancing the night
away" captures not only the density of the crowd and its
frenetic mood, but the sweaty heat. All three young men in
the foreground are bare-chested and at least one has been on
drugs. The evidence stares out from the dilated pupils of his
eyes.

Below the *Guardian*'s Hanger 13 report, there's news of
Sunday morning's death at the Mirage in Windsor. "There
have been about 50 ecstasy-related deaths in Britain, some
caused by youngsters taking substances sold as ecstasy,
which have included vitamin pills and dog-worming tablets.
The A-class drug, which is sold in tablets costing £10-£15
each, is widely counterfeited. But the genuine article can
cause the body to overheat, particularly with hours of
strenuous dancing."

The paper produces one or two statistics. Last year,
Customs seized enough ecstasy to make 2.3 million tablets.
In the north-west of England, a survey of 750 14-19 year-olds
showed that one out of every 10 had taken the drug. But
according to a Fellow of Manchester University who is
looking into drug consumption among the young, ecstasy
may be declining in popularity as the rave culture wanes.
Other hard drugs are more popular. LSD, for example, was

used by one in four of the teenagers questioned for the English survey.

A woman with a pale, gentle face is crying: we haven't had tears until now. Helen Dick, 43, mother of Andrew Dick, of Possilpark, Glasgow, only heard of her son's death when she reported him missing to the police. "I thought he was going to one of they places doon the toon. When Andrew never came home on the Sunday, I thought he was staying with a girl in Paisley. It wasn't until Monday that I 'phoned the police." He had been dead since 11.30 the previous night.

Unknown to his mother, Andrew Dick did not go clubbing in Glasgow that weekend. Instead he and his pals hired two taxis to take them 30 miles to Ayr. They arrived at Hanger 13 around 10 o'clock, instructed the taxis to wait, and agreed to rendezvous outside the club at 2am for the journey home.

Details of these travel arrangements are given in a deadpan way by a 19-year-old girl, unemployed, and corroborated by a 16-year-old boy, also unemployed. Andrew Dick himself was out of work. A question that no one considers worth asking is where all the money's coming from to finance this Saturday night jaunt down the coast. The witnesses appear to find nothing remarkable about it; the court listens without comment – yet the economics are baffling.

I asked a Glasgow taxi operator how much it would have cost Andrew Dick and his friends to hire two cars to Ayr, wait four hours, and return to the city. Let's assume that their estimate of £200 is about right. Let's further assume that there were five passengers (the maximum allowed) in each car. Here, then, is the least that Andrew Dick could have spent on his last night:

Share of taxi	£20
Admission to Hanger 13	£9
One bottle of water	£1
One ecstasy tablet (say)	£15
Total	£45

One witness remembered Andrew as he waited in the queue to be searched for drugs. He was "happy, jumpin' aboot, couldnae wait to get inside for some GBH."

"GBH?" Sheriff Gow is puzzled by the use of this foreign legal term denoting Grievous Bodily Harm.

"He said it was a kind of ecstasy."

"Was the term familiar to you?"

"I'd heard of it, know what I mean?"

"Did he say what the drug did for you?"

"He said it was amazin'."

Another witness recalled Andrew later in the evening. Now he was "fu' o' it, no' in a stable way, fu' o' drugs, just walkin' aboot hissel." Somewhere else in the hall John Nisbet was even further gone. Both youths were drifting into unconsciousness and both were alone. Outside, meters ticked over.

The first ambulance arrived at 12.30am for John Nisbet.

Ambulanceman: "A male had collapsed. I found a young gentleman who was being supported by two security guards. He was quite delirious. He was throwing himself about and could not be restrained."

The second ambulance arrived at 2.25am for Andrew Dick.

Ambulanceman: "Patient unconscious. Possible drugs. We found him outside, propped up against a wall. We tried to rouse him, but there was no way we could get any response."

Scott, 21, from Airdrie, tells the inquiry he is a frequent attender at Hanger 13 and buys from a regular supplier. He doesn't know who the supplier is; all he knows is that the guy is always there. The night the ambulances called for John Nisbet and Andrew Dick, Scott approached the guy but demand had been high: he was sold out. Scott got the stuff from somebody else – the first person he asked. Back home, his fingers became tingly, he began to hallucinate, he felt sick. They took him to hospital and put him on a heart machine. And this was after one tablet. Had he taken ecstasy since? Yeah, a few times.

Jack Drummond (Andrew Stoddart's uncle) asks Scott if the door search is tough. Scott thinks so. Then, how come the pushers manage to smuggle drugs into Hanger 13? No explanation.

Stephen steps into the witness box. Like most of the others from Glasgow, he is unemployed. I note: "Must be 12 years old." But he's older than he looks. He gives his age as 20.

"After you bought the tablet," the fiscal asks, "did you consume it?"

"What do you mean?", the witness replies. He has not understood the question.

"Eat it or swallow it?", the fiscal persists.

He knows what it means to eat or swallow. He does not know what it means to consume. *We do not love the young enough to teach them what it means to consume.*

Wednesday

> *The experts have told us of the dangers and a lot of us have experienced them. What you do when you're so overjoyed dancing but you find you can't really breathe properly. Your legs start to feel rubbery and you need to take a five minute break. You are so hot and no matter how much you drink, you can't cool down. You start to panic which makes your breathing worse and causes your racing heart to pump even faster. What kind of happiness is this?*
> – Lucy, Clydebank, in a letter to *M8* magazine

Four months after the funerals of John Nisbet and Andrew Dick, Hanger 13 was still open and more popular than ever. On 20 August, in the Lanarkshire village of Rigside, it was Derek Hamilton's birthday. He organised a bus to take himself and 14 friends, including Andrew Stoddart, to Hanger 13. They met at the local pub, the Viewfield Tavern, where the bus picked them up around 7.30. They made two brief stops: first to collect a tape from somebody's house, then to buy drink from an off-licence.

Lorraine, 18, machinist
Were any drugs taken on the bus to Ayr? – Not that I know of.

[Pause] *Do you know what a joint is?* – Yes. *Did you see a joint on the bus?* – Uh, huh. *And was it smoked on the bus?* – Uh, huh.

Lorraine and her pal Clare, Andrew Stoddart's girlfriend, stayed on the bus to change before joining the others in the queue. It was Lorraine's first night at Hanger 13 and she found the heat overbearing. She wasn't offered drugs; nor did she take any. For much of the evening she sat in the foyer where the air was slightly cooler.

Later, back in the hall, she saw Andrew Stoddart. He looked unwell. He was sitting on a chair. Clare was with him. Next thing she knew, a bouncer was dragging him to the doors.

Sheriff: "Could he walk?"

"He wasn't given a chance to walk. He was just dragged to the doors."

"Were you told what was going on?"

"Somebody said he'd be OK in a few minutes, that he was just dehydrated."

"Was there water to drink?"

"The water was turned off in one of the toilets. The pressure wasn't strong in one of the others."

At 4.15am, after the police had noted the names of everybody inside, the party from Rigside was driven to Ayr Police Station and told that Andrew Stoddart was dead.

Stewart, 17, warehouse assistant

This witness took an E on top of "Bud" (Budweiser). No after-effects.

"I don't suppose there's much happening in Rigside on a Saturday night," Sheriff Gow says out of the blue.

James, 19, unemployed

Said it was as if Andrew was having a fit. They got him out of the building and round the corner to a play park. He lay on the ground and the bouncers tried to resuscitate him. He was sick. They turned him over on his side. It started to rain. It was raining heavily. They called an ambulance.

Clare, 18, student

They seem a decent lot, the reckless kids of Rigside. There is a curious poignancy about the details of one wild night in these tender lives so brutally laid bare – the detour to pick up the tape, the carry-out, giggly girls changing into party gear in the back seat, even the hash passed down the bus as it bumps and twists along the old road to Ayr through Douglas and Muirkirk and other has-been places where God-fearing men once hid in the moors and prayed for deliverance. And now the most surreptitious event in this country of Covenanting graves and abandoned pits is an illicit puff of cannabis resin on Derek Hamilton's birthday bus to Hanger 13.

And Clare, pretty Clare, might be the nicest of the lot. She has been waiting to give evidence since 10.30 and now it's almost 1 o'clock. She is crying openly and nothing will console her – not even the comforting words of Neil Gow, who is skilled at putting the inarticulate at their ease.

"Please sit," he says kindly, and asks the court officer to fetch her a glass of water.

Painfully, the story of her evening with Andrew Stoddart unfolds.

When you got inside Hanger 13, he went away and came back, is that right? – He showed me three tablets. *And did he say something about having got three for £45?* – Yes. *And did you see him taking any of these tablets?* – Yes. *Right away?* – Not long after. *He took bottled water with the tablet, is that right?* – Yes. *When did he take a further tablet?* – Can't remember. *Did he offer you one?* – No. *You didn't want one?* – No. *So he took two. What did he do with the third?* – Don't know. *How was he after he'd taken the tablets?* He told me he wasn't feeling well. He said he had very sore legs. He had to go and sit down. *He had difficulty controlling his legs?* – Yes.

She called a steward and Andrew was taken from the hall.

"Was he conscious?"

"You couldn't really tell."

Sheriff Gow says that will be all; she can go now. She's still sobbing.

Craig, 18, unemployed

In the pub before they left Rigside, Andrew asked him if he would share an E. Craig agreed. It was normal to take an

E before a rave. Andrew swallowed his half while waiting in the queue outside Hanger 13. Inside the hall, Craig gave Andrew £60 and asked him to fetch some. Andrew returned with four tablets for Craig. "If you just walk about in there, people point you in the right direction."

Later, when Craig went to the toilets, there was no water coming from the taps. He was sure about that. What state was he in? "I wasn't aware of what was going on." But one thing he did remember. He remembered a girl screaming.

We have heard all we are going to hear from the punters. Now it's the turn of the pros. And for a spot of light relief, the afternoon session is something of a bouncers' outing. The press lose interest and by 3.30 I'm on my own. But I think the press are wrong. Bouncers are a species of minor anthropological interest.

Bouncer "A"

Kelman, the fiscal, ventures in his usual gruff manner a definition of a bouncer – except he prefers the euphemism "door staff" – as someone who is employed to regulate persons entering a venue and supervise the behaviour of those attending. But how do you become a bouncer? "Anybody can come down and apply," the witness assures him. Sheriff Gow has taken his wig off; maybe he's planning a career break. Anyway, if you're lucky enough to land a job at Hanger 13, you're taught how to search and resuscitate the punters and you wear a nice new uniform of white shirt, black trousers, and security jacket. And you look about as under-cover as the Rangers defence.

"Well, you can never totally stop drugs going in. We're not allowed to do internal searches."

"Have you ever seen drug-dealing going on?"

"I've thought I've seen something on quite a few occasions."

The sheriff wonders if the "general behaviour of the young people is satisfactory". It is. There are seldom any fights. That's all right, then.

Bouncer "B"

Jack Drummond: "Do you consider a staff of 20 stewards is

enough to cover a crowd of 1,200?"

"Definitely."

"You know there's a drug problem?"

"I suppose some get in. The police canny stop it, so there's no' much chance o' us stoppin' it. Quite a few have it stuffed up their backsides."

Bouncer "C"

Kelman is reading from a set of guidelines for the operation of raves prepared by the Advisory Council on the Misuse of Drugs. He's curious to know if the management has provided a "cool environment" where ravers may recover their breath. "Well, there's the toilets. But anybody short o' breath can go ootside for the breeze aff the shore."

Drummond: "We've heard evidence that a considerable amount of drugs is sold inside."

"I wouldn't know about that."

Sheriff Gow's deceptively light touch often yields surprising dividends. He decides to probe the nature of the rave scene: a lot different from anything else, the witness agrees. For one thing, ravers dance more. But you get ravers of all ages. People in their 30s and 40s have been known. Even Kelman looks mildly surprised by this revelation.

Bouncer "D"

What happens if drugs are discovered? "If it's a large amount, the police are called. If it's a small amount, they're flung out and the drugs are stamped on."

This is an astounding piece of evidence. It is not denied that an illegal drug is widely available in Hanger 13, yet what happens if punters are caught in possession of it? At the discretion of the staff, they can be reported to the police – but not automatically. No one challenges the wisdom of this approach or demands to know if the police approve of it.

Only Jack Drummond stirs up any aggro. All afternoon he has been nagging at his favourite theme: the thoroughness or otherwise of the search. Are members of the staff searched? It transpires they're not. Confronted by this flaw in the system, some of these mean hombres become a shade tetchy. It doesn't take much.

After the court rises, Sheriff Gow invites me to his chambers for tea. This could be awkward, but we scrupulously avoid discussion of the case. Instead he expatiates upon his hero, James Boswell, a fellow lawyer who considered the sheriffdom of Ayr such a sinecure that he thought of applying for the job. He might not consider it much of a sinecure were he around now.

We are to have tomorrow off.

Friday

> *Drug squad bosses were yesterday quizzing a*
> *schoolboy after a £5 million heroin bust. The 14-year-*
> *old was arrested in a massive undercover operation. A*
> *16-year-old boy and two men were also held over the*
> *five kilogram seizure in Glasgow's Kelvingrove area.*
> – Report in today's *Daily Record* (10 February 1995)

Dr Leo Murray, the first of the medical witnesses, is head of the accident and emergency unit at Ayr Hospital, but might not be for much longer. The local health board is considering whether to close the unit.

He's a big man with a bushy beard and he's wearing brown corduroy trousers. He talks too quickly for my moribund shorthand; his speech has a pace which seems perfectly suited to his profession. He describes the collapse of the human body as a headmaster might deliver an unfavourable end-of-term report.

They called him from home to attend to John Nisbet. When Dr Murray arrived at the hospital, the patient's pulse was extraordinarily fast, he wasn't responding to pain, he was very hot, his brain wasn't functioning normally. Suspecting ecstasy, Dr Murray contacted the national poisons service for advice.

Andrew Dick was admitted later that morning – "an exact re-run of the earlier patient".

Then, in August, Andrew Stoddart: "Clinically this young man was dead when he arrived. I was struck by the fact that his muscles were rigid. We were unable to open his jaw. We tried to stimulate an already dead heart. There was no response. He felt hot to the touch. I declared this man dead at 1.20am."

Andrew's dad is in his usual place, stalwart and impassive.

The fiscal produces a paper from a medical journal on the use of ecstasy as a mood enhancer and dance drug. The discussion turns technical. "Put it in simple terms," Sheriff Gow urges.

Dr Murray explains that normally our body can cope with heat: think of the effect of the sun as we lie on a Tenerife beach. But if we're jumping around at a rave in a high ambient temperature, and we've just popped a pill, and we're not replacing fluid, there comes a point at which the body's ability to control its temperature at 37 degrees fails. Our system breaks down with profound results. We start to bleed spontaneously. Clots develop all over the body. We're wrecked.

When Dr Murray graduated in 1979, he had never heard of ecstasy. Its use is now so widespread that he accompanied the ambulance service to a rave – not Hanger 13 – to observe the phenomenon for himself. He saw "hundreds of people" with widely dilated pupils.

Sheriff: "And the reaction to it will vary from person to person?"

"As with most drugs."

"Perhaps," the sheriff muses, "the most disturbing aspect is the possible long-term psychiatric effect."

"It could be," Dr Murray replies, "that, when you take this drug, you're either going about your business in a few days or you're dead. We don't know if there's a long-term effect yet."

Dr Ruth Adamson, 37, consultant pathologist, Crosshouse Hospital, Kilmarnock

Placid-looking woman of shy composure who spends a significant part of her professional life examining dead bodies.

"Complete breakdown of the body's functions," Sheriff Gow is noting from case papers on her post-mortems. "Breathing...heart... kidney...blood clotting..."

"That's right," she murmurs reassuringly.

Towards the end of her evidence, the sheriff picks up a gratuitous detail from her report on Andrew Stoddart.

"You spotted a tattoo on his arm with the word Scotland. Why did you note that?"

"Well, we usually note that sort of thing."

"Because you might be criticised if you didn't?"

They exchange knowing smiles.

Dr John Oliver, 50, senior lecturer in toxicology, Glasgow University

His analysis reveals how many milligrams of ecstasy per litre of blood the victims had in their bodies. But the readings are of limited value: it is impossible to deduce how many tablets they represent. The toxicologist does impart one alarming fact: the white dove weighs 300 milligrams, of which 60 milligrams are ecstasy. We are left to wonder what the rest might be.

"Ecstasy is far from the harmless recreational drug that many of its users believe it is?", Sheriff Gow asks rhetorically.

"It is potentially lethal."

"So what is your advice to young people?"

Dr Oliver gives an honest but pedestrian answer. Afterwards, outside the court building, he is interviewed by the BBC and asked to elaborate. Taking ecstasy, he says, is like playing Russian roulette. On all the bulletins that night, he is quoted as having "told the inquiry" that taking ecstasy is like playing Russian roulette. But he didn't tell the inquiry any such thing. Rather he shared this arresting metaphor with a reporter from the BBC. Does the distinction matter? Only as a minor illustration of the true purpose of the hearing, which is not so much a judicial inquiry as a health education campaign conducted via a pliant media.

Detective Constable Donald Fraser, 41, of Strathclyde Police drug squad is the star turn after lunch. His sardonic outlook and laconic humour appeal to Sheriff Gow.

"You have street experience?"

"I have been on the streets for 19 years."

"Today, however, you are wearing a suit."

"It is very nice to wear a suit sometimes."

"But you're still wearing your hair long, I see."

"Old habits die hard, m'Lud."

Between these droll exchanges, the detective gives a short history of ecstasy. It has been around since 1914. It is also known as MDMA and by the slang expressions Adam, Eve, X, and XTC. It was originally taken as an anti-depressant. In the late 70s/early 80s, it was banned in the United States and Britain.

"I take it," says the sheriff, "that the drug is manufactured commercially?" (Now, what might have led him to that surprising supposition?)

"No, sir," Fraser replies. "It is made illegally by pill machines. People with chemical knowledge can make up the drug in tablet form. It can be made up locally."

Kelman: "Is it a rip-off scene?"

"If you approached me, I could pass you anything and you wouldn't know until you took it whether it was genuine. Approaching someone in the street is the last resort. Users either have a regular dealer or a friend who does."

"Is the drug addictive?"

"No, sir. The dependence is psychological. Users can't have a good time without it."

"So they don't need the drug on the other six days of the week, when they're not at a rave?"

"Correct. They associate it with a particular environment. Ecstasy is a social drug."

More than any other witness, it is this beat cop who articulates the seductive appeal of ecstasy. As a stimulant, the drug increases the energy of the ravers so that they are able to dance for as long as five hours without a break. They feel euphoric: happy with themselves and others. And they are at one with the music: "they can hear the sound waves hitting their chest".

Sheriff: "Do most people at raves take drugs?"

"Not 100 per cent. I would say 50 per cent. And not always ecstasy. Other drugs too."

"Speed, perhaps?"

"It's cheaper, but the effects last for a shorter period."

"We've also heard about something called GBH."

"We believe this is an American drug. We have not seen it in the UK yet."

(A minor unsolved mystery: if this drug has not been seen in the UK yet, why was Andrew Dick looking forward to buying it in Hanger 13 in April 1994?)

"So," Sheriff Gow sighs, "this is a new worry that lies ahead."

"There is always something new on the horizon, sir."

"Do you ever get violence associated with ecstasy?"

"I have never seen a fight."

"So young people taking ecstasy are not a problem for the police?"

"Quite, sir."

Up to a point, m'Lud. Up to a point.

Two local MPs have arrived – George Foulkes (Labour), who has demanded the closure of Hanger 13, and Phil Gallie (Conservative), who believes that the club should stay open in order to prevent the drugs problem being driven underground. Each of these opposing positions is respectable, although Gallie's self-appointed role as apologist for Hanger 13 is surprising considering his zeal on other law and order issues.

Our masters hear a Mr McBride, the club's "PR consultant", outline his duties. "I look after the VIPs and any press," he declares. Hmm. Quite a chore.

Sheriff Gow chips in: "What sort of VIPs?" As a VIP himself, the local beak may be wondering why he hasn't had an invite. Or is this mere mischief from the Bench of a sort that Boswell himself would have savoured?

The answer is a treat: "They range from MPs to football players." Perhaps that range is not as wide as the witness makes it sound. It may not be wide at all. We're all showbiz now. Even Sheriff Gow with his statement to the cameras has become a small part of the global entertainments industry. Still, here is an unlooked-for bonus: who might they be, these anonymous MPs who have been hanging loose at Hanger 13? The question is unasked. There are limits.

Instead the sheriff lets the witness off the hook.

"You haven't asked Max Clifford along?"

"Not yet." Ho, ho. "They're just people we know in the business. All areas of society. People who come down to have a look, and we make sure they have a good night." One can imagine.

Sheriff: "There will be particular reasons for having these guests?"

The reply is nothing if not candid: "It's a PR stunt."

His employer, Fraser McIntyre, 21, is next. Describing himself as the manager of the Ayr Pavilion, he insists that the venue is known as Hanger 13 only on Saturday nights; there are other forms of entertainment on other nights.

Sheriff: "But on Saturday night, it's a rave."

"A dance night, we call it."

"And are you aware of a problem with drugs on the premises?"

"After the incidents, that would be fair to say."

He selects his words as carefully as one might select fruit from a supermarket shelf: all customers are searched before entering; searches, while thorough, necessarily stop short of the powers granted to the police; all stewards are first-aid trained; since the death of Andrew Stoddart, two paramedics and an ambulance have been in attendance and video cameras installed; posters warning of the dangers of drugs are displayed. As to water pressure in the toilets – he agrees there was a problem one night (the night Stoddart died, it so happens), but it was a failure of the public supply outwith the management's control.

Kelman: "Are there rest facilities in a cool environment?"

"There are areas within the club which are slightly cooler than the main dance hall."

"We have heard from the stewards that outside the hall is what they consider a cool area."

He nods.

Jack Drummond, the amateur advocate with a knack of unsettling witnesses, niggles this one by referring to Hanger 13 as a rave. McIntyre repeats that it is not a rave. Drummond is unrepentant.

"We have heard that the stewards and bar staff at your rave are not searched."

"That's right. We feel that our procedures for selecting staff eliminate any problems of that nature."

At the fag end of the week, it is left to Sheriff Gow to put the question that has been intriguing some of us for months: "Why did you call it Hanger 13?"

McIntyre: "It was to do with an aircraft hangar in the United States which supposedly held UFOs."

Wan smiles all round.

Week 2: Monday

My whole life changed after that first ecstasy. For the better. Yes, that's right. To me, Es make people love each other in a brotherly way. So, please explain to me what is the harm in that?
– Gary, Aberdeen, in a letter to *M8* magazine

While we've been away, it has been business as usual at Hanger 13. This morning, in another courtroom, four young people appear on drugs charges relating to incidents at the club over the weekend. Among them is a girl of 20 who is accused of possessing ecstasy with intent to supply. In the press benches there are cynical jokes about the embarrassing coincidence of these arrests.

The proprietor, Christine Ridha, 48, who is listed as a company director, corroborates the evidence of her son, Fraser McIntyre. It is hard to know what to make of Mrs Ridha. She appears reasonably pleasant and capable. She would not be out of place administering an office or teaching primary schoolchildren. Instead, here is this respectable middle-aged woman grotesquely miscast as an organiser of raves and superviser of bouncers.

Drummond: "Do you feel that, having charged £9 at the door, you have to charge a further £1 for water?"

Ridha: "I have no problem with that."

Drummond: "We've heard that water is essential."

Ridha: "I am supplying an entertainment venue, not a place for taking drugs. I have to pay for my water, and I think the price is reasonable."

Sheriff Gow evidently agrees that it is proper to charge for water. He wonders about the ventilation of the premises, but suggests that a full air-conditioning system would be expensive. Mrs Ridha says the possibility is being considered.

Sheriff: "Dancing in a warm atmosphere is part of the scene, I suppose? They don't expect to be dancing in the freezing cold?"

Nor, however, in a sauna.

At the end of the world, there will be a policeman like Detective Chief Inspector John Corrigan surveying the debris and preparing a report for the procurator fiscal. He isn't a bit like dour Taggart. He is relaxed and congenial. And he doesn't proceed in northerly directions either. He is a modern copper.

When Corrigan does a job, he does it thoroughly. He knows exactly how many people were present in Hanger 13 the night Andrew Stoddart died: 1,288, including 39 staff. And of those, Corrigan's men failed to trace and interview only 80. The others were systematically sought out and questioned.

"One of the largest investigations ever conducted in this area," Corrigan says. "To have spent 10,000 police hours on one inquiry is quite extraordinary."

And so, here at the end of the world, with all evidence spent, we are left with a two-page summary of one night in Hanger 13:

Home addresses given by persons leaving: Glasgow, 330; South Ayrshire, 319; North Ayrshire, 234; Renfrewshire, 153; Lanarkshire, 132; Dumfries and Galloway, 34; Lothian and

Borders, 14; Central Region, 7; England, 4; Tayside, 3.

Age of customers: 13 years, 2; 14 years, 3; 15 years, 31; 16 years, 72; 17 years, 107; 18 years or older, 1034. (To summarise: 215 – 17 per cent of those attending – were under age).

Number of people suspected of dealing: 25.

Number of reports to procurator fiscal: 14.

Number of prosecutions initiated: 6.

This is an impressive document: but it is not quite complete. Two further estimates may be relevant.

Gate receipts: 1,249 x £9 = £11,241. Multiplied by 52, this would yield an annual revenue for the Saturday "dance night" (a.k.a. rave) of £584,532. Caveat: the management claims that the average attendance is less than 1,249.

Illegal revenue generated by the 25 suspected drug dealers based on the assumption that 50 per cent of those attending take one ecstasy tablet per night at an average cost of £13: £8,112 (£324 per dealer). Multiplied by 52, this would yield an annual illegal revenue of £421,824. The same caveat applies.

The sheriff orders a 15-minute break before interested parties address him. In the corridor, Jack Drummond and Andrew Stoddart are looking glum. They feel the Bench has been unsympathetic to Drummond's line of questioning. They no longer expect much from this inquiry.

So to the closing speeches. Kelman, for the Crown, briefly summarises the evidence and commends the media coverage. He cites in particular the "Russian roulette" reference and acknowledges that he had listened to it on TV. He believes the inquiry has exposed a major drugs problem and "it is to be hoped" has highlighted the dangers of taking ecstasy.

Reid, for Hanger 13, maintains that all reasonable precautions were taken and that there were no management defects which could be said to have contributed to the deaths. "No search will ever be foolproof. We have heard no evidence that the staff had any involvement in the supply of drugs. It is clear indeed that the staff were not involved." Nor was there any criticism of staff reaction to the various incidents.

Drummond criticises the lack of a cool environment within the club, the ease with which drugs could be obtained, and inadequate stewarding of the large crowd. He reiterates his belief that all bar staff and stewards should be searched.

Sheriff Gow goes away for a long think about everything.

Wednesday

The sheriff enters a packed house dramatically late. So many have turned up for the verdict that extra seats are required. Mrs Ridha is here with her son and several of the bouncers. Of the families, only Andrew Stoddart's relations appear. And, of course, there's the press, more than ever.

Copies of the judgement are to be made available later, but I note what he says just in case.

Until a lapse at the end, it is written in lucid, elegant prose, is admirably concise, and marshals the evidence skilfully and fairly. But it is clear – it has been clear for some days – that the Hanger 13 management will emerge relatively unscathed.

He describes as "an obvious point of weakness" the failure to search staff, but notes that the manager was content to rely on the trustworthiness of his employees. "These are matters which should be left to the discretion of the management, and I have no particular recommendations to make."

Likewise, the chances of detecting surreptitious drug deals "might be enhanced" if more stewards, possibly out of uniform, patrolled the hall. But he stops short of a recommendation to this effect; again, the management knows best.

Furthermore, the club had "to a greater or lesser extent" met the recommended criteria for raves although "there may need to be air conditioning or the like in the longer-term". Meanwhile, the Scottish Office should promote model conditions for raves governing such matters as numbers, stewarding, and searches, "so that there is a clear framework within which to operate".

Sensing, perhaps that his judgement may have come as an anti-climax, Sheriff Gow offers the press a small bone. "A dance with ecstasy," he finishes with a flourish, "can lead to a dance with death." It's a headline grabber: my colleagues are well satisfied. But now, it seems, we have outlived our usefulness. A court officer announces that only six copies of an abridged version of the judgement are available. Either we share them – which means a scrum – or we pay £10 a head for the complete text. There aren't many takers.

The sense of unfinished business is deeply frustrating: this inquiry has raised as many questions as it has answered.

Here are three:

1. Why were those found in possession of small quantities of an illegal class "A" drug not reported to the police? Did Strathclyde Police give tacit approval to this policy? If so, why?

2. In the light of the management's claim that there was a failure of the public water supply on the night of 20 August 1994, why did the Crown not call an official of Strathclyde water department to substantiate the complaint?

3. Similarly, why did the Crown not call expert evidence on the quality of the ventilation?

We don't know the answers. I doubt if we ever shall.

Epilogue

A week has passed. Already, public interest in the case has evaporated. Phil Gallie MP says "nothing new" emerged; he believes Hanger 13 will now succeed in its appeal against the licensing authority's decision to revoke its licence. And the media caravan, a notoriously restless vehicle, has moved to fresh grief.

In Rigside, the grief is no longer quite raw. The Viewfield Tavern, where Andrew Stoddart and his mates met before the minibus picked them up for the visit to Ayr last August, has few customers this lunchtime. It's a fine little pub – it used to be the doctor's surgery until the doctor built himself a new surgery next door – with a horseshoe for luck, G & T for £1.28 and faded pictures on the wall of Rigside football teams.

An old man picks off the names. "Geordie Cranson," he says affectionately, "and Willie Forsyth, and Tommy Somerville, oh, and there's the doctor, Burns his name was..."

This is fertile footballing country. Ian St John started with one of the local teams and there are relatives in the village of the legendary Bill Shankly, who said that football was not a matter of life and death but something much more serious. And then I remember that Andrew Stoddart – a midfield player for Douglas Water – was part of that great unbroken heritage, so proudly alluded to by old men over slow half pints.

Football in the pit villages of Lanarkshire has survived even the industry which brought them into existence. The mine in Rigside closed so long ago that Andrew's dad can't remember exactly when. He thinks it might have been 1968. Now there's open-cast mining just off the main drag to Lanark, but they haven't excavated much of value. The monks got there first, and took most of the goodness.

Now, here at the back of beyond, there is just a petrol station, a social club which used to be the miners' welfare, a police station, a couple of shops, and a council scheme which includes too many houses abandoned and boarded-up. Travelling bakers and butchers call regularly, buses infrequently.

A haulage firm in the neighbouring village of Glespin – "blink and you miss it", they say in Rigside – provides most of the work that's going. Young Andrew Stoddart worked for this firm, as his grandfather had before him. He was fond of his grandfather and enjoyed a weekly drink with him in the Viewfield Tavern. Then, on 30 July 1994, the old man – though, at 68, not old – died suddenly. Andrew took it badly. He was inconsolable. Three Saturdays later, Andrew himself was dead.

All this is being explained to me in a warm, sociable living room at 17 Craiglea Street where Andrew lived with his parents, Andrew and Mary, his older sister, Deborah, and his younger brother, Stewart. Jack Drummond has joined us with his wife Anne. And the family parrot is observing the scene, though not saying much. Mary has prepared sandwiches, scones, cakes – and in the best tradition of Scottish hospitality, there's too much of everything.

Andrew is here, too, in an unexpectedly powerful way. He is here in the minds and the hearts of the people who loved him. He is seldom far from the centre of the conversation.

Jack: Andrew enjoyed life. He'd do anything for people. I never knew a more generous young guy.

Anne: When he came into a room, it was as if the room lit up. And I've got tears in my eyes again.

Andrew snr.: He was a hard worker. His job involved long drives to the north of England, 12-hour shifts, up early in the morning, back late at night. No complaints. When he had a night off he'd go football training, or work out in the gym at Motherwell, or maybe just watch TV. And he enjoyed drinking in the Viewfield. I'll say that for him...Andrew loved his drink!

Jack: And a good carry on.

Andrew snr.: But drugs...we had no idea. He didn't go regularly to Hanger 13. Only when it was somebody's birthday.

Jack: His pals called him Star.

Andrew snr.: Aye, Shining Star! We never knew why. When he died we got 230 cards of sympathy, and that's not counting all the letters. You should have seen the wreaths at his graveside up there. All the boys came to see us.

Jack: Young men were walking the streets, crying freely.

A few days later, Jack Drummond telephones. Have I seen the papers? A sheriff at Ayr (not Neil Gow) has postponed the hearing of Hanger 13's appeal against the loss of its licence. Meanwhile, the club is organising a "Save the Hanger, Save the Scene" protest dance, with Phil Gallie MP as guest of honour. A disc jockey billed to appear at the event has his invitation withdrawn at the last minute after his comment in the new issue of *M8* magazine that "drugs can be fun".

The appeal against closure will be heard on 21 April. Meanwhile, Hanger 13 stays open.

But not for much longer. The venue closed shortly afterwards, the Piv now lies empty, and Phil Gallie lost his seat at the 1997 General Election.

The treatment

On the road with the BBC

The lunch

The BBC called from London with an offer of a commission too enticing to refuse, even by a journalist who had vowed never to appear on television again. Here in essence was the proposal: I was to be given a free hand to make a short film about modern Scotland, a personal view of my country. "An essay" they called it. And, what's more, I was to be paid for it.

One of the conditions did make me hesitate. The state of the nation would require to be summed up in no more than seven minutes. But then I thought: if the Bible manages to report the creation of heaven and earth in a few crisp lines, even Scotland should be containable within seven minutes. I remembered from newsreading days that the regulation BBC speed of delivery is the equivalent of 180 words a minute; by this reckoning the "essay" – by which I took to mean the sort of superior feature which masquerades under that name in the posher papers – would allow me up to 1,200 words.

OK. To use the cant of the trade, I would go with this. As far as lunch at Television Centre, anyway.

White City, home of BBC Television, is one of the grimmer districts of London. It is not particularly sordid or threatening, but the blank wasteland depressed the spirits on a boiling day in high summer. I wonder where the staff in this characterless district manage to get drunk. Perhaps they don't get drunk. Certainly the programmes look as if they have been made by people who are very, very sober.

A lift took me to a floor high above London. In these quasi-celestial corridors "News and Current Affairs" reside. I was hoping to bump into Charles Wheeler, who has always struck me as fairly human by BBC standards, but instead I bumped into Kirsty Wark, who used to be fairly human too. I'm not sure about her these days; one can never tell what fame does to people.

"What are *you* doing here?" was her, not unfriendly, greeting.

"Well," I said, "a cat can look at a queen."

Ah, no. In truth, I found myself asking her to write for my wee magazine, the *Scottish Review*. It is a tactical error to ask broadcasters to write for small magazines; usually they offer the lame excuse that they are too busy – "fully stretched" as the great Lord Reith ambiguously put it. Only one broadcaster in my experience gave an original reply to such an invitation, and that was Donald MacCormick. He replied: "I'm not sure I have any writing ability." Later he proved to himself and the readers of the *Sunday Times* that this modesty, though not false, was misplaced. I should ask him again.

Kirsty, however, said, "I've got an awful lot on at the moment", and promptly disappeared into a room of fully stretched telly executives.

There were a number of other familiar faces from the past. One of the nicest and cleverest young producers at Queen

Margaret Drive in the late seventies, Tim Orchard, is now in charge of Sir David Frost's grand appearances on the Sabbath and the daily *Breakfast News*. There, too, was Liz Elton, who is married to Donald MacCormick, and Andrew Maywood, another of my former colleagues at Beebus North Britannicus, while MacCormick himself was said to be "in the studio".

"What interests me," said Tim over lunch, "is the way I sense things are different in Scotland now, the way the mood has changed since the last great devolution debate."

I am less sure about this; but I see what he means.

Did not our dear judges, after all, give the BBC itself a bloody nose for attempting to sully Scottish screens with a Prime Ministerial interview three days before the municipals? The same crimson robes then instructed whatever they call British Rail these days to continue the night train to Fort William, though why anyone should want to go to Fort William, even in the middle of the night, is a continuing mystery. Some prefer Mallaig, but these are qualified masochists.

But the Edinburgh Bench, aye that Bench which is located in the very place where the Auld Sang was sung for the last time in 1707, had stirred at last, and this was a matter of national surprise and mild rejoicing. For any improvement in the political self-respect of Scotland will not be brought about by the Labour sheep who graze apathetically upon the lowlands of that slumbering central belt, so-named because most of its inhabitants have been belted into submission. It will be brought about, as it was brought down 288 years ago, by the will and example of the Scottish establishment.

As the mineral water flowed, Tim explained that a polemical essay – it had become polemical now – was not a normal part of the *Breakfast News* agenda, but that he was keen to experiment with more adventurous journalism. As far as he was concerned, I could within reason say what I liked, go where I chose, and take as long as I needed to make the film. A reporter's dream.

The first draft

I returned to Scotland and began work on a treatment for the film. We will start with the One O'Clock Gun for three reasons: (1) it represents a certain type of Scottish cliché familiar to English visitors; (2) it will awaken any viewers the programme has managed to attract; (3) it gives the misleading impression that something exciting is about to happen in our failed capital.

I will then think of something suitably polemical to say.

From there we will move – this being August, the month of instant colonisation – to the streets of Edinburgh and shots of comic singers and miscellaneous pissartistry. "The Festival is a great party," I will observe, "but it's not *our* party. Maybe we, the Scots, are just the boring neighbours, invited along to keep us sweet." Always get the paranoia in early.

Then there's Glasgow. I will quote the Blessed Billy Connolly, who said that the city which was once etched in gloomy ink is now painted in bright colours. An evocative image taking us neatly into an extract from *Rab C. Nesbitt*, the flipside of the new Glasgow.

"Although Nesbitt is a grotesque caricature of the urban personality" – is this polemical enough? – "the people responsible for it are Scots. But they are Scots with a commercial eye to a wider market – the English market which rather enjoys having its prejudices about Glasgow confirmed. Is this really how others see us? No wonder the London *Evening Standard* imagines that our new Secretary of State has been banished to what it calls 'the Celtic fringes'. Watching Nesbitt, it feels more like the zoo."

Now we cut to what I will call "the real Scotland" – the home of the *Scottish Review*, Irvine by the sea, with its facilities of leisure centre, branch factory industrial estate, covered shopping mall for the plebs, and Development Corporation HQ in one of those splendid mansion-houses miles from town. Picture it if yous will.

"It's a Scotland which functions but fails to sing, a dependent community vulnerable to influences outwith its control." You can say that again; but, since we only have seven minutes, let's not bother.

We have, just around the corner from my bolt-hole, a cobbled street, symbol of the old town which was here long before they decided that Irvine was born yesterday. Burns worked in a sweat-shop in that street. It's a museum now. I will claim that Scotland is a country of too many museums and that it's time we led a vigorous life in the present.

This feels like the moment to take the viewer inside Galt House, named after our local novelist, not that the English will have heard of him – we would rename it Kelman House for the day were it not for certain philosophical and literary objections. In this, the publishing cottage of Carrick Media, Linda G. in a new summer frock will pretend to be compiling *Who's Who in Scotland* while I remark upon the number of people in our reference book who claim to be running Scotland but admit to being born in England. I will allege that Scots are sore about this, not because they are suffering from English influence but because there is so little Scottish influence left to inspire them.

I visualise now an interlude of purest mischief. At Edinburgh Waverley we will watch the Sunday night sleeper wafting our heid-bummers south, but not before they have changed into a pair of freshly pressed striped pyjamas. They are off, ambitious chaps that they are, for another week in a proper capital where serious decisions are made. The journalists, however, buy one-way tickets. They're no' comin' back, the bastards.

I will adopt a sad face and lament the ease with which people in my own trade are culturally absorbed into the metropolitan establishment, and allow themselves to be lured into such un-Scottish activities as cricket and grand opera. I will claim that 30 years ago I decided I wasn't joining them. This is not strictly true, for it never entered my head. Never gave it a conscious thought. Besides, nobody asked me.

I see myself in one of those sleeper cabins, a prisoner in a reception cell. A few minutes before the automatic doors close on Scotland, I leap up and cry, "Don't start this train! I want tae get aff, pal!" I rush to the door and hurl myself from the carriage.

A whistle blows. The train slides out of the platform. And I'm left standing there like one of Jock Tamson's bairns, jobless, hopeless, disenfranchised, and quite possibly the worse for strong drink.

The BBC, if I speak nicely to them, may give me a sleeping bag for the night.

Next morning I am magically transported to Glasgow Green. They're still repairing that crumbling monument. The winos are in their usual spot. Over there in the High Court, some desperado is about to go down for eight years. I shall talk of the young James Watt and the morning in 1754 when, walking on the Green, he chanced upon his steam condenser.

"Emotionally" – the polemicist strolls in the morning sunshine with nary a steam condenser in sight – "emotionally, I visualise Scotland as a small country which is still capable of the big idea. [Theatrical pause.] Maybe I'm kidding myself."

Next, Govan. Or, maybe, Motherwell. Or any of a hundred other locations which tell in stark pictures what I am going to say about the death of Scotland.

"Our inventors seem to have gone as silently as our vanished industries. When so many of talent and ingenuity emigrate, and this process continues unimpeded for generations, something valuable will inevitably be lost. What's at stake, as more and more vital energies are concentrated on London, is nothing less than the national consciousness of Scotland."

I think we'll shoot the judges now. We'll film Parliament House, where laws are no longer made but administered. And I will suggest that what we have been seeing recently may be a sign of a growing impatience with London arrogance.

I guess there will be library film of that room in the old Royal High School, the one they had prepared for the Assembly before we funked it in the devolution referendum.

Sixteen years later a semi-Scot called Blair says he will give us a second chance. When canvassers with clipboards stop us in the street and ask us if this is what we want, most of us say yes. I will wonder aloud how seriously – how sincerely – we mean it.

I am unable to resist a concluding shot from Calton Hill, icon of the unfinished capital. From here I can imagine the oil running out in this decade as the shipyards closed in the last; I will say that we are a perplexed race, frustrated yet curiously indifferent to our fate; but then I may turn to face the handsome city, and the Scotland that lies beyond; I will say that from here, provided we don't move a foot to the right, it is just possible to remember that Edinburgh was once a capital – and could be a capital again.

And then, it will be back to the suits in the studio: time for the stock market prices and the weather.

I faxed the draft.

The second draft

In London, they quite liked the script. A producer called Simon called to say that there were just one or two things. There are always just one or two things.

Simon was surprised that there were to be no interviews. It is true that, at an earlier stage, I had contemplated a sound-bite from Magnus Linklater ("a small price to pay for a great Scottish writer"). But then I dismissed the idea on the grounds that this was supposed to be a personal view of Scotland, and that Magnus isn't me.

Simon confessed that without talking heads the pictures would have to work hard.

"But the words, Simon, the words," I murmured.

"Oh, the words are fine," he said.

In the script I had mentioned that you couldn't buy a decent book in Irvine. Simon wondered if there was anything else you couldn't buy in Irvine.

I only care about the absence of books; it tells you a lot about Scotland, this dire lack of bookshops. I mean, it wouldn't surprise me if you couldn't buy a suit in Irvine either, but it is the unimportance of books that seems scandalous. I said I would try to think of other things you couldn't buy in Irvine.

Then he said that I had failed to explain why I was still staying in Scotland. The candid answer would have been that, like incest, Highland dancing and driving a car, leaving Scotland was something I had never got around to doing. But it was a fair criticism; I would have to explain myself.

Perhaps, having abandoned the train, I would make a short statement along these lines: "Scotland is my country. Why should I want to live in somebody else's? But then I have to ask myself another question: what's left to stay for?"

And I thought: this is as true, or not true, as anything else I feel about not leaving Scotland. The best lack all convictions. At least, I hope so.

The dinner

Simon came by air, while the others – cameraman and sound recordist – drove from London. What an exodus it is, this annual August flight to northern climes. Only this year the climes are not so northern, but fiercely hot, and hairy tattooed creatures with bare disgusting bellies have claimed the known world. We have lost all physical dignity and restraint. How swiftly we have degenerated under a cruel sun. And these are just the Scots, slipping effortlessly into Third World persona. But, lo, we have the whole of London here too. May the Lord in His mercy henceforth cancel August.

We agreed to meet – or, as BBC people do, rendezvous – in Lochgreen Hotel, Troon, and Simon gave me the bad news before dinner. Problems, we have a few.

My early morning walk to work through Irvine Mall has been postponed until the afternoon, the owners of the emporium having decreed that it must be after lunch or not at all.

A more serious difficulty has arisen with a Mr Foley,

principal clerk to the Lord Advocate, over our request to film inside Parliament House. Mr Foley at first refused to countenance such a daring idea because the political sentiments I was expressing might be misconstrued as being those of the Lord Advocate. After a week of haggling, we have finally secured a conditional agreement to film long shots in Parliament Hall, but under no circumstances must I *say* anything.

There is worse.

A body called Historic Scotland is obstructing our proposal to film up at the Castle. Is this the lot M. Magnusson chairs? It appears it isn't. The heritage bureaucracy is vast, and Historic Scotland a new one on me. As custodian of the boring protuberance, it approaches its duties with a proper seriousness. The deal is: we may film the One O'Clock Gun, but Roy may not deliver a piece to camera on the premises. Like Mr Foley, Historic Scotland is determined to avoid being linked in any way with the seditious text.

Ah, it was ever thus. But as Alan Watkins said in another connection, these days it seems to be thusser. In this abject province, rendered innocuous by three centuries of administration by people with rolled-up umbrellas and rolled-up brains, journalists are considered dangerous. It is almost flattering. But what does all this say about our masters' assessment of the democratic intelligence? Can a television audience not be trusted to distinguish between what is plainly one man's opinion and the corporate opinion of Historic Scotland, in the unlikely event that Historic Scotland allows itself to have an opinion about anything that matters much? Does Mr Foley really have sleepless nights about telly presenters making vaguely nationalistic noises because they could be mistaken for those of the Lord Advocate himself? Who is the Lord Advocate, anyway? How ridiculous must we allow ourselves to become?

But we didn't talk much about the ridiculousness of Scotland in Lochgreen Hotel that night. We talked about the BBC. Simon said my opinion of John Birt was reductionist.

The shoot
Day 1

I am converting this account to present tense. Tense it certainly becomes. They arrive at the office 40 minutes late, they being Simon, Sam and Philippa. Sam is the cameraman. He sports trendy shades of perfect roundness, as cameramen under a certain age do. Philippa, the sound recordist, meditates and lives in Islington. Simon is a thin young man with a back pack.

It is decided that Linda G. will not be filmed in her summer frock pretending to compile *Who's Who in Scotland*. Only I will appear in this scene. I'm rattled. The film I see in my mind's eye is already slipping away. And it's hot, bloody hot. But cools are kept. Just.

Once outside, the real fun begins. I am asked to walk a short distance from the street into the office, talking to myself as I enter the building. Simon calls this unnatural behaviour "impromptu".

"Well, here I am, going to work in Galt House. It's named after a local novelist, but you probably haven't heard of him. He's been dead a long time."

"That was good," Simon says. "We've got to get the audience to *love* you."

Sam doesn't fancy the shot, though. Something to do with the light. We'll try again, when the light is better. But we never do. I am destined never to be loved.

My colleagues have cleverly arranged with the manager of the Granada TV shop for every set in the window to show a video of the Nesbitt programme. The extract ends with a head-butt. I am to look disapprovingly at this scene, turn from the bank of TV sets, and deliver a piece to camera about the nature of the "real" Scotland.

It's 4.30pm.

Take 1

"Well, so much for the sick joke. But this is the real Scotland...Irvine, a new town 20 miles south of Glasgow..."

Two malevolent youths lurch into shot. "Hey, we're frae

the Irvine Casuals. What's goin' oan here? Who're you, mister?"

Take 2

"Well, so much for the sick joke. But this is the real Scotland...Irvine, a new town 20 miles south of Glasgow..."

"Sorry, Ken, fluff on the lens."

Take 3

"Well, so much for the sick joke. But this is the real Scotland...Irvine, a new town 20 miles south of Glasgow..."

A small boy breezes past me doing an excellent piece of mimicry. "Well, so much for the sick joke," he parrots. "But this is the real Scotland...Rab C. Nesbitt."

Take 4

"Well, so much for the sick joke. But this is the real Scotland...Irvine, a new town 20 miles south of Glasgow..."

This time it's a tannoy announcement which begins: "In the interests of safety..."

Take 5

Cue village idiot.

Take 6

A woman in the crowd asks if I'm a star.

Take 7

Cue screaming weans.

Take 8

Cue guy with trolleys.

Take 9

Shutters come rattling down over the shop next door.

Take 10

Polemicist is certified clinically mad.

Now we must drive to Edinburgh in order to see the sleeper depart. Although rooms in the Mount Royal Hotel have been booked for the crew, no accommodation has been arranged for the mad polemicist, it being commonly understood in London that Scotland is sufficiently small to permit all its inhabitants to walk home from wherever in the country they happen to be. A tiny joke is made of the oversight; a spare billet is secured.

I call room service in the Mount Royal Hotel.

"I'd like a round of cheese sandwiches, please. Oh, and a glass of dry white wine."

"Dry white wine?"

"Hmmm."

"I'll see if we have that."

Room service goes away and comes back.

"Yeah, we seem to have that."

"Oh, good."

At 10.30pm, we go to the office of Railtrack in Waverley Station for a "safety briefing". Railtrack's representative, a man of such earnest demeanour that I assume he is sending himself up, asks Simon to sign an indemnity form, reads out an extensive list of dos and donts, and warns me, when I attempt a slight jocularity, that he reserves the right to ask questions about these important matters.

The others leave to set up the shoot.

Out on the platform, a festive atmosphere has been generated by the presence of a camera. People look awfully pleased to be leaving Scotland, I must say. One young woman positively dances on to the train. Sam asks her to do it again for the camera, but she isn't as natural a second time.

A distinguished middle-aged man – he could be an academic or a doctor – agrees to be filmed inside his cabin.

"What's it all about?"

"I'm doing this film about Scotland and what a hopeless state we're in, basically."

"Certainly under the present Government," he replies.

"What's going on?" another asks.

"We're making a film for the BBC."

"Oh, congratulations," he says sourly.

The train sequence works well, though my "Don't start this train, I want to get off" line is judged almost risibly corny. "*Very* Leslie Neilson," Sam says, and my colleagues break into knowing laughter.

"Isn't he a Yorkshire murderer?"

Uncontrolled hilarity.

The train has gone and I rather wish I was on it.

"They wanted you to blow the whistle as it left," I remind

ScotRail's ambassador on the platform.

Softly, conspiratorially, he replies: "*Fuck the whistle.*"

The shoot
Day 2

Another day in paradise, also known as sub-tropical Edinburgh. In eager anticipation of this adventure, I bought in York last week, from a shop called Gap, a light shirt of deepest blue. Simon insists that in the interests of continuity I wear the same clothes for all pieces to camera. It seems a bizarre request, for it must be clear to the dimmest viewer that the entire film has not been shot on the same day. However, I am complying. The shirt has been hanging out on the window ledge all night.

After breakfast we trudge up to the Royal Mile and I go off on my own for a bit. A man is washing graffiti from the wall of the High Kirk of St Giles. The message is: "Stop nuclear test's. Don't buy French." Soon it is wiped clean away.

And I think: an aberrant apostrophe spoils a good case; why is he expunging such an impeccably Christian sentiment?; this lot would have barred me from doing a piece to camera inside – they are the spiritual equivalent of the Foleys and the Historic Scotlands. And then I think: the film we are making is not the film we should be making. We should ditch the pre-conceived schedule and respond to what we see around us. We won't.

The Castle is a hell-hole of buses, honking horns, and sweating tourists. The whole world is here with its rucksack and its camcorder, and soon the glorious tale of a warrior race will unfold in the nightly charade of the Military Tattoo. Meanwhile, flunkies in tartan trews guard the gate. They have badges bearing the dread words "Historic Scotland" and the first who opens his mouth speaks in the historic twang of deepest Essex.

Simon wants a fix on the gun, so that we can pull off the blasted cannon for a piece to camera down in Princes Street. The chief flunkey recommends Debenhams. We go to

Debenhams.

A delivery man from Scotsman Publications lifts a hefty load of Edinburgh Evening Newses from the back seat, bangs the door, and marches off looking like thunder, and that's take 1 scuppered. By the time we're ready for take 2, the venomous vendor is back for more Edinburgh Evening Newses and more banging of doors. Heavens, what a popular paper.

After these and other extraneous interruptions, we finally get one in the can.

Simon strokes his chin thoughtfully.

"Think you could make it a bit more...you know...chatty-ish."

"*Chatty-ish?*"

"Yeah. Just a bit."

He still wants the audience to *love* me.

I leave them to film the Gun. In my absence there is a nasty scene on the rock. Sam is all set up when someone from the Army arrives and tells them to shove off. Permission from Historic Scotland? Not worth the paper it's written on, old boy.

It is 250 years almost to the day since Charles Edward Stuart raised a standard at Glenfinnan. Some marched south with him. Two battles were won. Then at Derby they turned on their heels and marched all the way back. Later, the English exacted a terrible revenge. Later still, the same English, being subtle strategists, lifted the prohibition on the wearing of Highland dress and the carrying of arms if the defeated clansmen would fight for king and country. Great regiments were formed, and the rest was tragic irony.

What's left? Just the Tattoo, and the indignities of international tourism, and a power struggle between a government department and the remnant of an army for administrative control of a visitor attraction. I suppose it's the nearest thing these days to a battle.

But I've missed all that. The man selling papers at the bus station, when I asked for the *Scotsman*, said: "How did I guess? An educated man like yourself. That'll be 42 pence for the paper, and no extra charge for the patter." Then a lovely waitress in the Mount Royal Hotel asked if I was "visiting or dining". I said that this sounded to me like an Edinburgh way of putting things, to which she replied that she came from a far far better place called Morayshire. Yes, I've had an enjoyable day in friendly Edinburgh. And now I'm sprawled on the grass on Calton Hill in baking late-afternoon sunshine, with a boulder for company and an excellent view of an ice-cream van. People are kissing each other all over the place, though mostly on the lips. It is really a most ardent scene.

Time passes.

Out of the shimmering heat comes the shape of a Range Rover. Soon little Philippa will be thrusting a furry microphone in my face or threading a much smaller one through my Gap shirt for clipping on my tie. Except I don't have a tie any more: the hell with continuity. There is yet another piece to camera to face and there will be many takes. They shoot horses, don't they?

To Glasgow in the evening. I am dropped in the city centre outside a dingy hotel selected for me by the BBC, while the crew head off to the pampered luxury of One Devonshire Gardens. Nice for some.

The shoot
Day 3

They're late again – I'm kicking my heels in reception from 8.15 in anticipation of an "early morning" shoot on Glasgow Green. The others show up an hour later, blaming the heavy traffic along Great Western Road. I am furious and show it. We drive in silence to the location where there is the usual pantomime about parking cars and humphing gear. And I think: let them get on with it.

Most of the benches are occupied by solitary old men staring into space. You get a better class of conversation here. Years ago, I joined one of the old men of Glasgow Green on his bench and we talked about James Watt and how the idea of the steam condenser had come to him during a Sunday morning stroll. I wondered if anybody on the Green had any big ideas any more, and the old man pointed to the high flats across the way and said: "Here's an idea. Why don't they pull that lot down and give the people somewhere decent to live?"

They didn't. I'm on the same bench again, looking up at hundreds of windows. But one thing I hadn't noticed before was the ugly factory next door, pouring a greyish vapour into the humid atmosphere. This is what people see from those windows. This is their immediate view of the world. And the sensory nightmare does not end there. There is also noise pollution to contend with – a loud, insistent hum from the industrial process which is conducted within. Perhaps the tower-dwellers, the people behind the windows, are anaesthetised to this obscenity; in that ghastly phrase which seems to tidy away all modern horrors, perhaps they have "come to terms with it".

"I don't know if we can do a piece to camera here," Philippa is saying. "That *din*." While they editorially confer, I wander off to speak to another old man on a bench. I ask him if there is a statue of James Watt on the Green. He rises, as if to attention, and replies with grave and humbling formality: "There is not, sir. But if you go to George Square, you will find a Watt monument there. It might be worth a visit to the City Chambers – it's in George Square, too – and they could give you more information about James Watt. Yes, sir, I'm sure they could."

I tell my colleagues where to find Watt's statue, just in case they're interested. They're not.

"Well," Simon says, "we'll have you standing there", and points to the spot.

"But it's a walking shot," I protest.

"No, we'll have you standing there."

"I'm talking about a man having a walk on Glasgow Green and you want me standing?"

We do a standing piece to camera, and then a walking piece to camera.

"You sound as if you've lost heart, somehow," Simon says.

"I'm talking about the death of Scottish industry and the emigration of our people. How do you expect me to sound?"

"No, what I mean is, your delivery lacks conviction."

So we do the piece several times more, until the producer is satisfied that the presenter has related the death of Scottish industry and the emigration of the people in a brisk, approved BBC breakfast manner.

By the time we're through, I have decided that the steam condenser wasn't such a brilliant idea after all. Had Watt never walked on Glasgow Green, the world would have been a happier place for having been spared the indecencies of industrial squalor. I am now writing in my head one script and delivering to camera another.

Afterwards, I escort Simon on a guided tour of the city centre. He sounds less than enthralled. He says Glasgow reminds him of Manchester. But then I show him Princes Square, and he perks up.

My part in the filming is over. They will spend the rest of the day doing general shots of this and that. Tomorrow we will edit the film and Simon says I am to be available for as long as the BBC requires my services – all day and all night if necessary.

The mad polemicist finally turns ballistic.

The film

We watch and wait. There's rather a lot about VJ Day. Jowly old Bernard Ingham, almost a parody of himself now, reviews the morning papers. Then, just after 8.30am, there's me – "a journalist explains why he isn't leaving Scotland". It is not at all bad. So smooth is the professional veneer that there is no hint of the parallel universe behind the making of these seven forgettable minutes. And at 8.37, it's somebody else's turn.

The Scotsman decided to re-publish this piece from the Scottish Review. For the purposes of illustration, I had my photograph taken. A life-size cardboard cut-out was then made from the photograph and carted around the various locations of the film. The resulting sequence of pictures proved to be effective, if slightly weird. Afterwards Maggie Lennon, the commissioning editor, asked if I wanted to keep the life-size cardboard cut-out. I thanked her kindly, but declined. She was then left with the problem of what to do with this clumsy artefact. I lurked in a corner of her office for a while, an object of some curiosity if not ridicule. On cold days visitors would hang a scarf around my neck, or lend me their hat. Then, one morning, Maggie Lennon returned to her office after the weekend and discovered that I had gone. No one knew what had happened to me; or rather no one was saying. I fear I may have come to a sticky end.

The same commissioning editor proposed that I should go to Linwood, where they used to make cars, and write a long piece about the death of the Scottish car industry for the Weekend Scotsman. I have never owned a car, and I do not drive. Furthermore, Linwood was scarcely the most enticing location. But I went, anyway, and was glad I did. So what comes next is Linwood.

Volkswagen of the glens

Linwood

31 January 1996

Robert, taxi driver, Paisley Gilmour Street station:

"It was a brilliant wee car! I had three of them. VHS 100 was the first. My uncle gave me it when it was nearly clapped oot. But I worked on it and got it goin' again. Well, it was just a basic car, but with the engine in the back it made for very light steering. And for a wee car it seemed to have plenty of room, even for a big guy like yourself."

We left Paisley, home of gun-toting drug barons, and entered a bruised landscape where the industrial poor of the west of Scotland once beheld the promised land. Eighteen years later, when the promised land had become an embarrassment, the vultures in suits observed a decent period of national mourning – not too long, of course – before erecting a trading estate on the knacker's yard of the

Hillman Imp.

With a fine regard for mythology, they called it the Phoenix Retail Park. Arise from the ashes, Discount Bike World! Arise, Arnold Clark!

"Look," said Robert, "the foundations and the internal roads are still there. Asda – that's roughly where the paint shop and the body shop used to be. See McDonald's? That was the press shop. And they built the bingo hall on the site of the boilerhouse. I'll take you across the road into the original factory. Big bloody place still lying empty. Look at it. Bigger than a toon."

He drove until he could drive no further, past cavernous shells once known as machine shops, slanted at jagged angles, with windows high in the roof. At the end of the road we came upon a building open to the elements, the only one they forgot to padlock. It had a notice of admonition on the door, a reminder of 1960s' industrial relations: NO UNAUTHORISED PERSONS ADMITTED. PENALTY INSTANT DISMISSAL.

We stumbled over pigeon droppings, rubble, scraps of old newspapers, cigarette ends, broken bottles – the thick soup of industrial dereliction – until we reached a room with most of the floorboards missing. At the far end there was an electricity switchboard. "Would you believe it," Robert said, "the power panels are still in place."

And for an absurd moment in this abandoned workshop, you felt that it might be possible to throw a switch and set the whole pitiless machine in motion again.

2 May 1963

A few weeks after the monarch visited the Glasgow slums and earned the *Daily Record*'s endorsement as "Queen of the Gorbals", her husband opened the Rootes plant near the 18th-century industrial village of Linwood. Pedants claimed that, strictly geographically, the factory fell within the boundary of neighbouring Elderslie, birthplace of Sir Malcolm Wallace, father of the patriot. This was the least of the misunderstandings which dogged the embryo Scottish car industry, and one of the few which failed to provoke a union meeting.

Later in 1963, a chivalrous Tory candidate called George Younger sacrificed his political ambitions in order to give the new Prime Minister, the 13th Earl of Home, a safe seat in the House of Commons. Meanwhile, the 13th Mr Wilson, Labour's pipe-smoking Yorkshireman in a Gannex raincoat, was turning over in his mind an election-winning slogan – something about the white heat of a technological revolution.

But why wait for the end of "13 wasted years" of Tory rule? In the West of Scotland it seemed that the revolution had already begun. The *Scottish Daily Express* sounded positively euphoric, as it tended to do in those far-off days when tabloid newspapers occasionally used words of more than one syllable. "A Scottish car right down to its hub-caps," it trumpeted, "and it's Scots who will build it. Now, isn't that refreshing?" Norman Buchan, the local MP, clearly thought so. "The factory will be a growth centre of immense importance to the whole Clyde," he predicted, "and will contribute to curing the cancer of Glasgow's housing."

Despite such stirring expressions of confidence, it was difficult to quantify the broader economic advantages. For Linwood to become a growth centre, it would require to attract supporting investment in the form of components suppliers and ancillary industries. Greenfield sites were provided, more in hope than in expectation.

But the social benefits were obvious at once. Two thousand new houses at Linwood were built for the car workers, many of whom had been recruited from the declining shipyards and coal mines. For these men and their families, 2 May 1963 should have been glad confident morning – escape from spent industries, the barbarous slums, a dark and defeated city.

Now, wasn't that refreshing? Evidently not. Three weeks later, Linwood went on strike for the first time. Shop stewards complained that the men's wages compared unfavourably with rates of pay at the company's main plant in the West Midlands. The strike lasted only 36 hours, but it was a discouraging augury. It had a sour taste of prophecy.

31 January 1996

The only bank in Linwood town centre has been closed for nine months. Customers are directed to the nearest branch five miles away. But the postman faithfully delivers the mail. "The future starts tomorrow", says a leaflet recently dropped on the mat.

In Ardlamont Square, once the commercial heart of the town, the public library is one of the few buildings still open. Scribblings on the wall:

Fuck the system; Fuck the proddys (orange bastards); BNP (British National Party).

Linwood Information Centre. 12.45pm.

Desk 1:

Woman, tired, late middle aged: mumble, mumble, council tax, mumble.

Advisor: Another £8 a month might keep them happy. Can you afford that?

Woman: mumble, mumble.

Desk 2:

Advisor: What exactly is wrong with your boy?

Man, tired, late middle aged: mumble, mumble, muscular spasms, mumble.

Advisor (sympathetically): There are only two of us on today, and this problem could take an hour to sort out. Would it be an awful hassle if you came back tomorrow?

Man: mumble, mumble.

Car park. 1.00pm.

Toyota. Volvo (badly rusted). Volkswagen. Vauxhall Nova. Mitsubishi. Fiat Panda. Nissan. Two Fords (battered).

Pub. 1.15pm.

Barman to customer: This place is all played out. Even Christmas Day wisnae up to much.

October 1964

In the month that Harold Wilson entered No 10, the first Scottish-made car since the 1920s was "rolling off the production line at the rate of one a minute" – a headline-grabbing claim, though not consistently true. The patriotic vehicle, our very own Volkswagen of the glens, was rather comic in appearance and some experts claimed to have detected a fundamental design fault. Nevertheless, it was exported to England in fairly large numbers and won a few rallies before it finally lost the battle. Good heavens, this was not so much a motor car as Scottish history on wheels.

Yet the Imp – renamed the Caledonian Imp when the going got desperate – was no more Scottish than its most buoyant supporter, the *Daily Express* – maybe less so, for at least that newspaper's proprietor, Lord Beaverbrook, could claim ancestors from that other vehicle-building centre, West Lothian. What could Lord Rootes claim, except an overwhelming and quite natural desire to recoup some of the £23 million he had staked on taking his company into the volume car business? He had not wanted to come to Scotland. Like any sensible motor manufacturer he had wanted to expand in Coventry, where he had offices, technical know-how, engine shops, the lot. The Government, Harold Macmillan's never-had-it-so-good administration of one-nation Toryism, persuaded him otherwise by stick and carrot.

Strange as it may seem to anyone born within the last 30 years, there was a time when Conservative governments not only had a regional development policy but were vigilant about enforcing it. Lottery tickets in the early 1960s were called IDCs – Industrial Development Certificates – which steered growing industries not to the places they necessarily wanted to be, but to the places of greatest need. By withholding IDCs for existing locations, the Government effectively forced the car industry to move to the north of England or Scotland.

Only Rootes was prevailed upon to gamble on Scotland.

The prototype of his Imp was capable of a top speed of 100 mph, but the noble Lord, given half a chance, would have quit Linwood rather faster. Peak production of 72,000 cars, achieved in the election year of 1964, was less than 50 per cent of theoretical capacity. Only 18 months after it opened, the plant was already operating a four-day week.

Industrial relations, never good, deteriorated sharply.

31 January 1996

Linwood Welfare Club. Posters for "Grand Domino Singles", "Arthritis Care", and "Lazee L rootin' tootin' entertainment".

Early afternoon. Pints, chasers.

Harry, who is 67, was a dye-setter in the press shop. He was employed at the plant from the day it opened in 1963 until the day it closed in 1981. He has a sad face and walks stiffly.

Colin, who is younger and sparkier, also worked at Linwood but is vague about what he did and refuses to give his surname.

Jimmy, bolshier and franker than the others, rolls his own cigarettes. He describes himself as a trim snagger.

Jeremy is a photographer who wants a cup of tea, but they only have one teabag in the Welfare Club. He settles for a soft drink.

And there's me, wondering about the lost art of trim snagging.

Jimmy: A trim snagger fixed all the wee faults with the motor before it left the plant. Maybe we'd build up a door or change the glass if the car was damaged.

Me (a non-motorist): Was the Imp a good car?

Harry: Don't know! Never owned one! But it was excellent value. Under £500 brand new and if you worked in the place you got a discount. Far superior to the Mini. More space. Pretty good small car. A lot of the higher-ups had one.

Me: Did people feel good about working at Linwood?

Harry: Most people. I'd been in the yards – Stephens of Linthouse – earnin' a tenner a week. At Linwood, on piecework, you could make 15 in a good week. That was money most of us hadn't made before. And you got a new house which went with the job.

Me: If most people felt good, how come there were so many strikes?

Colin: There were a few stupid strikes, sure, but a lot of times we were laid off because of other people's stoppages. We got a bad name for things we didnae do. We were never as black as we were painted. It boiled down to the quick buck...Governments making huge investments, management pulling the plug.

Me: Are you angry about it?

Colin: (sighs) It's a very long time ago to be still angry.

Me: You were a shop steward, Jimmy, one of the baddies.

Jimmy: You're kiddin' of course. They hadn't a clue, that management. Nae consultation. Once we started to make real money the first bonus was 12 quid a month. Very good money. Then it went doon tae 11, then 10. By the finish it was 30 bob. Hey, wait a minute. They were includin' everybody in this bonus, even the shithouse clerk. One month we got 10 pennies. Auld pennies in they days. Stuff it up yer Jacksies!

Harry: One month we owed *them* money!

8 June 1968

But whose Jacksies? There was no point any more in stuffing it up Lord Rootes's jacksies, for his company had been acquired by the American motor manufacturer Chrysler, whose UK management swiftly alienated the Linwood workforce – no great accomplishment in itself, except that the new kids on the block achieved alienation on a scale impressive even by Renfrewshire standards. The workforce, shedding their reputation for four-hour stoppages about nothing very much, stayed out for a month over a disputed productivity plan.

Even the *Scotsman*, a paper of moderate temper and almost infinite patience, grew slightly restive towards the end of the strike. The 1967 by-election victory of Winnie Ewing at

Hamilton had inspired the vision of political autonomy. The question was: were we up to it?

"The rights and wrongs of the present dispute have become almost impenetrable," an editorial acknowledged. "But the details are less important than the persisting lack of responsibility shown by Rootes workers towards their industry, which in Scotland is a frail plant. If the growing spirit of nationalism is to have a positive content and lead to political self-government, it must include a realisation that industrial democracy (and profitability) are as important as a Parliament in Edinburgh. Opposition for the sake of disruption, a refusal to attend a meeting because it involves crossing a road in the rain – that kind of destructive obtuseness widely shown would put Scotland beyond redemption by its own Parliament or anything else."

Twenty eight years later, I read the paragraph to the men in Linwood Welfare Club.

"Aye," Jimmy responded sourly, "but what did the (Daily) *Record* have to say?"

"This *Scotsman* paper," said Colin. "Does it have a racin' section?"

A persisting lack of responsibility towards their industry. I asked them if it was true. The little group looked thoughtful for a bit, then Colin said: "I don't think there was any guy in there who didn't feel responsible for the job he was doing." The others nodded.

"That's not quite the same thing," I suggested.

They looked to me as if to say: "Well, that's how it was, pal."

23 April 1969

On a day of brilliant sunshine, Barbara Castle, Labour's Secretary of State for Employment, went by helicopter to the Linwood plant to defend her unpopular policies for trade union reform. The management, fearful of a rough reception, waved her to a waiting car, but the old trooper turned and walked towards the crowd. A young apprentice leaning over the wire called out: "Give us a kiss, Barbara." "Of course," she replied and held up her face. A roar of delight went up. It set the mood for the day. Only a few booed.

Any day in the late 60s

Eight thousand workers were now employed at Linwood. The newspapers developed a lazy habit of referring to the car industry as a symbol of Scottish industrial regeneration, a description which disguised the grisly truth. Losses were £2.5 million a year, sales sluggish, the supporting investment had failed to materialise (those greenfield sites remained greenfield), management was inept, the workforce volatile and unhappy – this was the underlying reality, barely acknowledged except when a crisis blew up, as it did with unfailing regularly.

Only the deep pockets and political will of successive governments, increasingly motivated by the fear of nationalism, kept Linwood open at all. "Give us a kiss". "Of course". And each time the Government blew a kiss it tended to blow another few million: an estimated £100 million in grants and subsidies before the game was up.

This was not industrial regeneration in any sense that mattered; it was merely the illusion of revival. But it was the orthodox view in Scotland at the time.

Such was the craving for imported genius and capital as an answer to the accumulated ills brought about by the collapse of our traditional industries, the Scottish Office failed to consider what the deliberate creation of a branch factory economy would do to national self-confidence and self-esteem. While the press adopted a high moral tone about the intransigence of the workforce, the real problem went deeper. Linwood's so-called "chief executive" was no more than a jumped-up plant manager forbidden to spend more than a few thousand pounds a year without written authority from head office.

There was another dimension to the Scottish illusion, a more profound self-deception. It concerned the faith of the

Lowland Scot in the power of the machine. This amounted to a form of worship. It took an Englishman, Rudyard Kipling, to understand the nature of our machine-idolatry. He wrote a poem about a Glasgow engineer, MacAndrew, a monologue in which the Calvinist Scot welded his engine to his God in a perfect union of the physical and the spiritual:

> *From coupler-flange to spindle-guide I see Thy Hand, O God –*
> *Predestination in the stride o' yon connectin' rod.*
> *John Calvin might ha' forged the same – enorrmous, certain,*
>   *slow –*
> *Ay, wrought it in the furnace-flame – my "Institutio".*

History is disorderly: the small car did not neatly succeed the great ship. There was a period of overlap; indeed it was during the lifetime of Linwood that the QE2 was launched with great ceremony from Clydebank. This was the last stand of Scottish craftsmanship, hail and farewell, baptism and funeral, in one glorious climax. After that there were to be no more connectin' -rods. Nothing connected any more. But the sad significance of the occasion took a long time to dawn on the national consciousness. We went on pretending to love the machine.

What died that day in Clydebank, and could never be re-born in Linwood, was the pride of the fitter in his individual skill, and a fascination with the world of ships and engines that by his own hand he had helped to create. Kipling sensed that it was not enough for these men to have made a product of little or ephemeral value. It must be a thing of beauty and nobility. It must be built to last. Furthermore, and essentially, it must pay. No wonder this was a craftsmanship forged by Calvin personally. Nae wonder.

And then we asked these same men to stand on an assembly line and make a silly wee car at the rate of one a minute. It was at this point – the actual point of mass production – that the Lowland Scot fell out of love with the machine and decided that he might as well be a waiter.

February 1981

Peugeot, the plant's third owners, announced that it was closing its Scottish operation in the face of growing losses. In the same week, the Labour-controlled Renfrew District Council put up council house rents by 55 per cent. The councillors simultaneously awarded themselves interest-free loans – to buy new cars.

To the dismay of the Scottish TUC, the Linwood workers rejected by 2-1 their shop stewards' advice to oppose the closure. As one union leader pointed out: "Few people here have any experience of winning." Margaret Thatcher was in power now; her Government's attempts to save the factory were half-hearted to say the least. Something important had happened: the gravy train didn't stop here any more.

22 May 1981

Scottish Daily Express:

"The car plant at Linwood closes today with the gates shutting behind the last of 4,800 redundant workers. And as the men turn away from the factory which has been a symbol of Scottish industrial regeneration for nearly 20 years, they will leave behind almost 3,000 cars in the compound and millions of pounds worth of machinery.

"The final car, a Sunbeam, came off the production line last Friday, and this week the workers have been getting their redundancy cash."

31 January 1996

Linwood Welfare Club. Harry and me.

Can you remember the date you were paid off?

You always remember the date you're paid off. 22 May 1981. Of course, we knew it was comin'. We'd known for weeks. Peugeot had taken over from Chrysler. They maintained that Linwood was too far away ever to be successful.

What happened on the actual day?

The senior foreman came round and said: "Right, that's it, lads." We were told to congregate over in the west area, where we used to eat our piece. Then everybody was told to go across the road to the south side, and there you got your cheque, and that was it.

How much did you collect?

£7,500. More than most. I think the average was about £4,000.

What did you do then?

Went to the bank with the money! Then had a drink. They actually did me a favour. I was 52, my family were grown up, and my wife was ill. I looked after her for 10 years till she passed away. I never worked again.

What do you think about Linwood now?

We have forgiven the people who sinned against us.

Who were the sinners?

Higher management.

20 November 1981

They called it "the sale of the century" when Linwood's plant and machinery, all 14,000 lots, went under the hammer of the auctioneer, Mr Butcher. Demonstrators protested that the multi-national owners, having received large sums of money to equip the plant, were now able to benefit a second time from its sale. The demonstration failed to hold up the auction. "Shouting is worth nothing," said one German buyer.

In the House of Commons, the Secretary of State, George Younger, cutting the same chivalrous figure as he had 18 years earlier, defended the Scottish economy from Opposition accusations that it had collapsed. But the dirty work of defending the Linwood auction he left to a junior minister, an accountant called Alex Fletcher, who said bluntly that the car industry was dead – a "relic" which had to be swept away. And so it was, leaving scholars to exhume its remains, years later, in academic tomes. Most agreed that a new factory with a new, ill-trained labour force should never have been asked to build a new car: that it had been an aberration, a massive failure of commercial sense, a colossal misadventure.

31 January 1996

Linwood Welfare Club.

"We'll never get decent pictures in here," the photographer whispered. So we persuaded Harry and Jimmy to return with us to what was left of their former place of employment. We got out of Jeremy's car at the end of the road and I pointed to the dreadful notice warning workers of the penalty for trespassing.

"Instant dismissal," Harry muttered. "Aye, there was plenty of that, right enough."

Jimmy said: "My God, how this place used to jump. Eight thousand men at one time, and now ghosts. Ghosts. The wreck of the bloody Hesperus, that's what it's like. You know, the toilets were so clean you could have eaten your dinner aff them. Some did."

The two old union men, having surveyed the wreckage, fell silent.

Then Jeremy said: "Tell you what. Walk away into the distance, and I'll take a picture."

And they walked away into the distance.

Nearly there!

A walk along Princes Street

Early in the reign of Harold Wilson, a very long time ago, I worked in a small office overlooking Edinburgh Castle. It was the heart of Scotland: a Princes Street window no less. From this incomparable vantage point the Scottish Council (Development and Industry) plotted the economic strategy of the nation.

Our leader, a Messianic kirk elder figure in a black suit, commanded a somewhat larger Princes Street window and a correspondingly larger vision.

He was fond of expounding two great theories:

1. The speed of change would become faster and faster. It would – to use one of his favourite words – "accelerate". He preferred to deliver this message on the move, restlessly pacing the executive floor. High above us, the Rock itself may have trembled at the prospect.

2. We must go on making things. In our manufacturing

base, our endless capacity for doing good with our hands, our inventiveness and our ingenuity, lay Scotland's strength and the key to its future.

I prepared many press releases propagating variations on these themes, one of which proved to be as correct as the other was disastrously wrong. The pace of change did indeed accelerate, but it swept away our manufacturing base and most indigenous enterprise with it.

It was pretty clear, even in 1967, that the game was almost up, that the world no longer wanted Scottish engines, and that our leader was deluding himself. A few of us persuaded the chairman, Lord Clydesmuir, to make a speech tentatively mooting the advantages of an alternative, service-based economy built upon such sissy un-Scottish activities as tourism, financial services and culture; so convinced were we by this unlikely scenario that we volunteered to write His Lordship's script. The subversive theme was anathema to our chief executive and of little interest to the Scottish press, which gave the speech half a column and promptly forgot all about the mythical service economy.

Yet, it has come to pass. Lord Clydesmuir, the first member of the Scottish establishment to spot our potential as a race of waiters, shop assistants and keepers of Tourist Information Bureaux, went recently to his grave, a prophet without honour. Look now at Princes Street, where our revolutionary script was written. Is it not the very apotheosis of our dream of a cleaner, better, more prosperous Scotland? Well, I shall walk the length of it and see.

Which Princes Street, though? There are two. There is the Princes Street of gardens and benches, ice cream vans and gentle recreation. Among the great European cities, Brussels boasts in its centre a statue of a small boy peeing, Amsterdam a museum of sex. Only in Edinburgh do you find a putting green.

This side, the Castle side, is also the Princes Street of St John's Episcopalian Church. On a grey, brisk Spring morning, its organ booms impromptu before a congregation of one, a middle-aged woman deep in prayer.

145

In the graveyard of the church, a young Australian is talking into a portable telephone. Behind her, a headstone commemorates the life of John Mitchell, surgeon, who perished in the Crimean War in September 1854, aged 45. "I'm a visitor to Edinburgh and I'd like to do some aerobics classes. Is there anywhere?" She is standing upon the last resting place of Thomas Laycock, Professor of the Practice of Medicine, Edinburgh University, who died a century before the technological revolution so eagerly anticipated by the Scottish Council enabled stray Australians to communicate with the outside world from a Princes Street graveyard. "Is that anywhere near the King James Hotel? Wonderful! Thanks for your help!" The service economy claims another satisfied customer.

I leave the unquiet graves of Mitchell and Laycock, put behind me rehearsing organists and aerobics enthusiasts, take a deep breath, face the roar of the traffic, dodge the oncoming Corporation bus to Fairmilehead, and cross in a manic fashion to that other Princes Street, the side devoted to mammon. And what do I find there? Walking slowly east: what used to be called The House of Binns but has been reborn as The House of Fraser; the Royal Bank of Scotland; the Bank of Scotland; American Express; the Edinburgh Woollen Mill; the Alliance and Leicester; BT; and, before long, the ubiquitous McDonalds with places for 110 upstairs and 75 downstairs.

SEATS AND TOILETS are guaranteed by a notice in the window. The modern world demands no less.

Then: Sports Connection; another Woollen Mill ("Closing Down Sale"); and Gap for Kids.

Outside Gap for Kids, a man is mixing cement on the pavement and shovelling it into a wheel barrow. Why is he mixing cement on the pavement? And what is he about to do with it? The manager of Gap for Kids remonstrates with him. She points out, not unreasonably, that cement-mixing is bad for business.

"I have my work to do," the man says in a matter-of-fact way.

"But must you do it outside our shop?"

"It's as good a place as any."

He promises that he will go in due course. He will take his cement to an undisclosed destination in Rose Street. But he is clearly in no particular hurry.

A few yards along, they are digging up the pavements outside HMV ("Closed for major refurbishment"). Four burly chaps embody something of the fraternal spirit of our vanishing working-class.

"I'm busy."

"So am I."

"Tough."

"Up yer fuckin' arse."

In Waterstone's, they have given over a window to a display of "Scottish Books of the Century"....."the top 25 titles by Scottish writers as voted for in the Books of the Century Poll." The book of the century is – surprise, surprise – *Trainspotting*, eight places ahead of *Sunset Song*. The execrable Irvine Welsh has two other entries in the top 25, Iain Banks eight, James Kelman two. No George Mackay Brown, no Eric Linklater, no Neil Gunn, no Iain Crichton Smith. The kindest thing you can say about this risible catalogue is that it displays an almost complete ignorance of 20th-century Scottish writing. It is hard to say which is worse: the mentality of the un-named panel of illiterate voters or the cynicism of the book chain's marketing department as it shamelessly plugs the results for all they're worth – which is precious little.

But I mustn't get upset. I mustn't. I have scarcely begun this constitutional along Scotland's most celebrated thoroughfare and already I am close to despair. Lighten up, pal.

Refurbished Offices To Let.

Virgin Megastore.

Ah, here's a Big Ishoo vendor billeted in the doorway of the Energy Centre ("Shop Relocation Sale"). Older than the usual. Less aggressive. Unlike his Glaswegian counterparts, he does not respond "Thanks a million, Jimmy" in a sardonic tone when potential customers pass him by. He seems quite a decent guy by Big Ishoo standards.

Music blares from Dixons. Garish shop sign.

BUY NOW, PAY 1998. Could this be Tony Blair's hidden agenda?

A teenage beggar crouches, head bowed, outside Burger King on the corner of Castle Street. "Homeless and hungry....Please help." His plastic cup overfloweth not. In fact, it's empty. Meanwhile, inside

THE HOME OF THE WHOPPER

an enormously fat woman in an orange blouse is eating chips from a paper napkin.

Burger King is the culinary equivalent of Waterstone's Top 25 Scottish Books of the Century. The power of the market and the educational system which have conspired to make *Trainspotting* the most popular book in Scotland for 97 years have also inspired such delicacies as

CHICKEN PICK EM UPS WITH CHOICE OF DIPS. 6 PIECES £1.72.

It is a grisly scene. The staff are fairly cheerful in a vacuous sort of way, but make no immediate attempt to clear abandoned tables littered with the remains of food. People smoke as they eat, lift the junk with their fingers, and drink from enormous cardboard cups full of dark, sticky liquid. If this masochistic activity was an obvious source of pleasure, it would not be quite so horrible a spectacle. But the customers look so sad, so doon in the mooth. For a few pounds more they could have chosen to eat cheaply and in some style at Pierre Victoire round the corner. Instead they have condemned themselves to this joyless experience: or perhaps it would be truer to say that they have *been* condemned, for these people have not been educated to expect or seek out anything better. It is the same the world over, I hear you say. But I am not concerned with the world over. I am concerned with Edinburgh, our capital and our hope, which might and should be a citadel of European civilisation.

What was here, in this spot, 30 years ago? I should be able

to remember, for across the street is my old office, above the Palace Hotel which isn't the Palace Hotel any more. There used to be a milliner called Mr French, that I do remember. There were many swanky shops and department stores in this street, until the locally owned businesses (with the honourable exception of Jenners) were frightened away or bankrupted by the high rates and philistine policies of Edinburgh bailies, all of whom somehow escaped long terms of imprisonment for what they did to Princes Street in the name of town planning. And do still.

Well, the Scottish Council (Development and Industry) has gone, to Glasgow rumour has it, if not yet to that great Trade Mission in the sky: where my former employer pontificated endlessly about the accelerating pace of change we have Biggar, Baillie and Gifford on the fourth floor, Castle International Asset Management on the fifth, Scottish Value Management on the sixth. I doubt if any of that lot has ever made a beautiful object in the whole of its deeply unattractive corporate life. What that lot make is only money, then some.

Tie Rack.

Vodafone.

Ravel. Not a composer, but a shoe shop – the fourth in the last 200 yards.

River Island.

Russell and Bromley. So help me, a fifth.

Two more beggars, a big woman laughing coarsely and a sly fellow with a decrepit dog. Cigarette butts litter these broad, once-elegant pavements: it seems the people who claim to administer Edinburgh are incapable even of sweeping the streets regularly. "Education, education, education," Blair said when asked last night on the telly what his party regarded as the priorities for Britain. This is no more than an empty slogan repeated twice, as politicians insist on doing for fear we didn't hear them the first time, but in any case it's not just about education, education, education. It's also about the state of the pavements.

Bargain Books.

Thorntons. Buy a chocolate bar in here. No eye contact with the girl behind the counter, who continues chatting to her mate throughout the brief transaction.

Cable & Co. How many more shoe shops does Edinburgh need, for heaven's sake?

"So what am I to do?" a woman asks her companion as they stop at the lights at the corner of Frederick Street. "Delegate my work to Mary and sit on my arse all day?" She is middle-aged and smartly dressed: she would not look out of place in a Morningside church choir.

The corner of Frederick Street is being rebuilt.

OPENING SOON. USC BRANDED FOOTWEAR.

Here, then, is the answer to my question of a moment ago. Of shoe shops, Edinburgh needs one more. At least.

Defying the bulldozers and the diggers, Hector Russell, Kiltmaker, remains open in his cosy tartan basement, the local headquarters of the Misplaced Apostrophe Society.

GENTLEMANS' HIRE DEPARTMENT

it says in one window.

GENTLEMANS' HIRE DEPARTMENT

it confirms in the other.

In order to entice/repel the customer – delete according to literary taste – Hector Russell has inserted a poem in his window display:

Noo mark ma words an pay great heed
Theres [sic] nae nead [sic] tae be a skunner [sic]
A lightweight tweed is aw [sic] ye nead [sic]
so come oan in an be a dandy for the summer [sic sic sic]

Upstairs, a Salvation Army man rattles his collecting can.

I have reached No. 90 Princes Street, approximately the age I now feel. This address is occupied by Crawford's Country Kitchen. On closer inspection, the Country Kitchen turns out to be nothing of the sort. It is a self-service, slightly chilly caff selling golden fried fillet of haddock, with chips, for £3.90. This Country Kitchen no more resembles the real thing than did that other marketing wheeze, the Ploughman's Lunch, which transformed the fortunes of thousands of grotty pubs 20 years ago.

Jeanster.

Barratts. I'm losing count of the shoe shops.

Mother Care.

Etam.

Saxone.

Clarks. This is a city of shoe fetishists. Mrs Marcos lives in Bruntsfield.

As the Hanover Street junction approaches, there is the first all-too-audible wail of Princes Street pipes. A tall young man of military bearing is strategically positioned outside the Royal Scottish Academy. He is playing a lament, and by God there's a lot to be sorry about.

A bucket of water has been chucked over the steps of the RSA, perhaps in a half-hearted attempt to drown the drop-outs who have taken up residence in its portals.

"Champagne!" they call out. "Champagne!"

A whippet answering to the name appears from the general direction of the putting green and races towards his masters. It is a strangely picturesque exhibition. And it's the only one we are likely to get in this vicinity all day.

GALLERY CLOSED

I push open the door, and am confronted by a caretaker busy with a sweeping brush.

"We're between exhibitions." Sweep, sweep.

Despite his show of industry, a curious apathy prevails. The exterior of the building is quietly falling to bits, but no one seems to have noticed. There are nasty slogans daubed all over the place, but no one seems to have noticed them either. And then, most conspicuously and nastily, there are the grungy folk with Champagne the whippet, as hideous a collection as you will encounter east of the reptile house at Corstorphine Zoo. But even they seem to be invisible to the nice people who run the RSA and who go on pretending that everything is all right really, when the truth is that something has gone horribly wrong on their own doorstep. This scene – this particular exhibition – needs an artist's vision to explain what has happened and why. The nihilism of a Welsh is no longer enough: not that it ever was.

Back, with some relief, to the shop side, where a young couple are gazing at engagement rings in the window of H. Samuel (what the H stands for is one of the abiding mysteries of the retail world), as young couples are still permitted to do when no one is supposed to be looking. Dolcis (the shoe joke wears thin, like even the finest leather sole), the Peoples Phone (not so much a misplaced apostrophe as no apostrophe), the Disney Store – every want catered for, every demand satisfied, up to a point. And opportunistic billposters are heavy with the promise of night.

DISCO INFERNO
FREAK – HOT DISCO
SCOOTER – INDIE BEATS
LOVE SHACK

Even Princes Street has to end somewhere. It ends with a fine flourish – but you will have guessed as much already – with a second Burger King.

I go on walking nevertheless, pausing only to use the fragrant lavatory in what was once the NB Hotel but is now the Balmoral, where Andrew Neil is said to hole up when he is not ruining/running the *Scotsman* (delete according to literary taste).

Here is the Scottish Office, or one of them. When I reported the affairs of our colonial department for Beebus NB in the 1970s, one St. Andrew's House was sufficient. Now there are three. A second and uglier lurks in the uniquely ghastly St. James development, while a third and more pleasing has been opened down by the Leith docks. When deevolooshun comes, doubtless there will be a fourth, if not a fifth. Then Scottish Offices will breed like Edinburgh shoe shops.

And now I come to The Vigil.

I had not hitherto visited The Vigil, though this is reliably said to be Day 1,832. It was set up as an angry, instantaneous, positive response to the General Election of 1992, the one in which Mr Kinnock pulled defeat from the jaws of victory, and has been sustained night and day ever since, by a group of hardy souls who support the cause of a Scottish Parliament. A poster has been printed with the latest good news. The fight is all but won. We are

NEARLY THERE!

[At this stage we had not had the 1997 General Election. Not quite.]

After 1,832 days, The Vigil has a nicely worn, homepsun, here-since-the-year-dot appearance. George Wyllie, the sculptor, has donated a wooden cannon which adorns the pavement; not sure what that is about. And there is a budgie in a cage, intended to symbolise the tartan tax. Not a real budgie, you understand. Maybe George Wyllie sculpted it, too. Am I missing something? Then there is a steaming hot brazier for toasting one's hands, or warming one's patriotic bottom, through all the dark nights of the soul since the Tories were returned to power.

NEARLY THERE!

Listening to the conversational tone of the three men in attendance, you have to wonder if the exclamation mark is not a bit over the top. They sound as if they have just returned from a funeral; and there is no doubt that the corpse in question is that of socialism.

The most striking of the melancholy trio is a grizzly chap sporting a natty waistcoat over a tartan shirt, a battered hat left over from some awful cowboy picture, and a pencil behind his ear. This colourful ambassador is framed in the doorway of the Vigil caravan, listening sympathetically as one of the others recites a long, distressing poem about the iniquities of life on the dole in an Edinburgh housing scheme.

"Very good," the third man nods when it is finally over.

"Very good," agrees the pencilled one.

The conversation turns to the lack of community spirit in the schemes and the divisive social effects of allowing tenants to buy their houses. "It sets neighbour against neighbour," argues one. "Makes him think he's better than the man next door." Murmurs of consensus.

And then it strikes me: I have left Princes Street and the new Scotland far behind. By the simple expedient of extending my walk by a few hundred yards I have landed in an older Scotland, the country of my youth, where men talked gravely of the importance of community spirit, knowing instinctively what it meant without having to describe it; a Scotland in which the tribe mattered and ancestral voices were heard with respect; a Scotland of the council house, the war memorial, the Co-operative gala day, the Burns Supper and the municipal playing fields named after some long-dead Labour councillor; a Scotland of the WEA, drama clubs, and mutual improvement; a Scotland, in other words, that no longer exists, has not existed for some time, and will not be brought back by constitutional change.

As I observe the innate decency and social concern of these men, the disturbing possibility occurs to me that what The Vigil has been all about – what *they* are all about – is not the future but the past; that 1,832 days have taken us no closer to defining the essentials of a more humane, creative and sustainable modern nation state, far less to a realisation of how to bring it about; that perhaps they – we – have not the energy left even to address such a matter. So we are left with questions. What will rescue Princes Street from its brutality, poverty and squalor? What will restore Edinburgh as a handsome capital of the arts, a model of some new enlightenment? What will make the new shoes worth wearing?

The Scotsman re-published part of this piece from the Scottish Review. I was amused to see the point at which it was truncated: just before the reference to Andrew Neil, the paper's editor-in-chief. So the shortened version contained nothing at all about The Vigil. It may therefore be said to have missed the point.

Labour went on to regain power, has enjoyed the luck of the devil ever since, and is resurrecting a Scottish Parliament in Edinburgh, opposite the new headquarters of the Scotsman. Meanwhile the former editor of the Observer is about to edit a new Sunday newspaper in Glasgow. History goes on repeating itself, though not always as farce.

Index